The Crown of Martyrdom

The greatest legacy Lincoln left to his party was the crown of martyrdom. In truth his great achievements were too big to be claimed as the private property of any party, though inevitably the Republicans staked their claim and could not possibly be prevented from enjoying some of the fame. But the two great achievements of Abraham Lincoln—what he did to save the Union, and what he did to defend and assert democratic government —transcend party, and indeed, in their remoter consequences, transcend his own country. Abraham Lincoln did more than any other single man to preserve the American Union, to remake the United States and to state in imperishable language the harder truths of democracy.

—From Chapter 13

MEN AND HISTORY

Collier Books ready or in preparation

Lincoln

K. C. WHEARE

(Originally published as *Abraham Lincoln and the United States*)

New York COLLIER BOOKS

First Collier Books Edition 1966

Abraham Lincoln and the United States *was published in a hardcover edition by The Macmillan Company.*

This title first appeared as a volume in the Teach Yourself History series under the general editorship of A.L. Rowse

The Macmillan Company, New York

PRINTED IN THE UNITED STATES OF AMERICA

Contents

Author's Note

IT IS NOT easy to write a short life of Abraham Lincoln in these days. There is at once too much and too little material. Lincoln's printed writings and speeches add up, according to the counting of an enthusiastic American scholar, to 2,078,365 words, which is more, he tells us, than either the Bible or Shakespeare. Upon this original foundation has been heaped an enormous and ever-growing mass of books and papers and pamphlets upon every conceivable aspect of the subject. They can be numbered by the ten thousand. That is one side of the problem. Over against it there must be placed the fact that not all the original material relating to Lincoln is yet available to the student. It was only on July 26, 1947, that the collection of papers desposited by Lincoln's last surviving son, Robert Todd Lincoln, in the Library of Congress at Washington was opened to the public. The collection contains about 20,000 separate documents, bound in 194 volumes, and it is obvious that their contents and significance cannot be appreciated by the student until some years have passed.

But the situation is not so desperate as it may appear. It is not presumptuous to say that, although the collection of Robert Todd Lincoln has been withheld for so long, and although it will undoubtedly reveal much that is interesting, none the less it is practically certain that most of what it is important to know of Abraham Lincoln is known already. John G. Nicolay and John Hay, the president's two secretaries, had access to all these papers when they wrote his official biography, *Abraham Lincoln: A History*, published in 1890. In the mass of secondary writing on Lincoln, little that is valuable is to be found. But that little is very good. It affords a sound and adequate basis, along with the printed records of what Lincoln said and wrote, for a short biography.

I have relied on the one or two great writers on Lincoln and on American history for the bulk of my information. I must mention in particular the works written or edited by Nicolay and Hay; the illuminating and fascinating *Growth of the American Republic*, by S. E. Morison and H. S. Commager; and, above all, the works of that great Lincoln scholar James G. Randall. My debt to Professor Randall, and in particular to his masterpiece of brilliant compression and information, *The Civil War and Reconstruction*, will be evident on every page. But he placed me still further in his debt when, in the spring of 1947, I travelled through some of the Lincoln country in Illinois, and had the opportunity of discussing with Professor Randall, at the University of Illinois, some of my puzzles and problems in the Lincoln story. Such kindness and patience from an experienced scholar towards an amateur is difficult to repay. I regret that, as footnotes are, naturally and properly, discouraged in a book of this kind, I have been unable to acknowledge fully my obligation to all those upon whose work I have drawn.

Few men can feel themselves adequate to the task of writing a life of Abraham Lincoln. It is a great and tragic theme, full of sentiment and sadness, of conflict and frustration, yet of courage and glory and of horseplay and laughter. One is tempted either to exaggerate or to minimise the dramatic and sentimental aspects of the story. I must confess freely that my own tendency has lain towards a bare and dispassionate narrative—as unfitting a treatment of the theme as those highly coloured and idealised writings which have contributed to the making of the Lincoln legend. Where I have attained to a proper balance between bare narrative and strong feeling, the credit must go most of all to those who have read my manuscript in its various forms and have urged and encouraged me to do better. I am particularly grateful to a distinguished Lincoln scholar, Professor David M. Potter, of Yale, who, to my great good fortune, came to Oxford in the academic year 1947–48 to occupy the Harmsworth Professorship of American History. He read the book in proof, and from his friendly criticism and advice I profited greatly. I would mention also two colleagues at All Souls College, Mr. A. L. Rowse, the General Editor of this series, whose confidence and criticism have been a continual inspiration, and Mr. Lionel Butler, who read my proofs with great care and patience. My wife has read the manuscript many times, and such style and clarity as the book displays owe much to her.

K. C. W.

ALL SOULS COLLEGE,
    OXFORD.
March 26, 1948.

Chapter I

Origins

"Thirteen sisters beside the sea,
    (Have a care, my son)
Builded a house called Liberty,
And locked the doors with a stately key;
None should enter it but the free.
    (Have a care, my son.)"
STEPHEN VINCENT BENÉT: *John Brown's Body*.

ABRAHAM LINCOLN WAS born on February 12, 1809, at a place called "Sinking Spring Farm," about three miles south of Hodgen's Mill in Hardin (now La Rue) County, Kentucky. The time and the place are significant. At the time of Lincoln's birth Thomas Jefferson was within a few weeks of the end of his time as third President of the United States. Yet Jefferson's Presidency was to influence the life of Lincoln. For it was in these years that there was inaugurated and established that Democratic party against which Lincoln was to work and fight throughout his political career and over which he was at last to be victorious. The Democratic party claimed Jefferson as its founder. It stood for the maintenance of the independence of the individual member states of the American Union, and for a restricted interpretation of the Constitution of the United States, more particularly where the powers of the Union government were concerned. It had opposed the Federalist party to which John Adams and George Washington, Jefferson's two predecessors, had belonged, and which had stood for the development of a stronger national government for the United States. With Jefferson's election to the Presidency in 1800 there began a period of power for the Democrats which continued practically uninterrupted, except for a term of four years, until in 1860 Abraham Lincoln himself was inaugurated as sixteenth President of the United States.

Lincoln was born in the state of Kentucky. The first thing to notice about the state of Kentucky is that it is a Southern state of the American Union. Lincoln was born a Southerner. His whole political career is associated in men's minds so exclusively with the North that this point is forgotten. It should not be over-stressed, of course. After all, Lincoln left Kentucky, as we shall see, at the age of seven and never lived afterwards in a Southern state. But he did live in states where Southern influences were felt, and his first seven years had made him open to them. He was to show himself alive to Southern attitudes and Southern views. He was to be called a Southerner on some occasions. He was said to speak, in mature life, with the Kentucky idiom. "Take it all in all," says J. G. Randall, "from his earliest breath to the public burdens of the fuller years, Kentucky was a part of Lincoln."[1]

The second thing to notice about the state of Kentucky is that it was not one of the orginal thirteen states stretching down the Atlantic seaboard. It was a "frontier" state. It had been carved out of those great tracts of land which, after the War of Independence, had been ceded by Great Britain in the treaty of 1783. These lands stretched northwards to the Great Lakes and westward to the Mississippi river, and they covered an area in which nowadays ten states of the Union, in whole or in part, are established—Minnesota, Michigan, Wisconsin, Illinois, Indiana, Ohio, Kentucky, Tennessee, Mississippi and Alabama. But at the time of Lincoln's birth it was still wild and undeveloped. Only three of these states had been organised, Kentucky in 1792, Tennessee in 1796 and Ohio in 1802. It is of fundamental importance in the life of Abraham Lincoln that he was born on the frontier. His grandfather, Abraham Lincoln, had moved from Virginia to Kentucky, then still a county of Virginia, about 1782. His father, Thomas Lincoln, had bought a farm, on credit, in 1808 near Hodgen's Mill, and it was in the log cabin on that farm that Abraham was born, and there he lived for the first two years of his life.

But Lincoln was not only born in a frontier state; he lived his whole life, until he became President, in frontier states.

[1] *Lincoln, The President*, vol. 1, p. 6. See the same author's *Lincoln and the South*.

When he was two his family moved to a better farm, on Knob Creek, eight miles from Hodgen's Mill, again purchased on credit. But in Lincoln's eighth year they were on the move again, and this time they moved out of the state of Kentucky into Indiana to the north. They reached Indiana in the autumn of 1816, and in the same winter Indiana became a state of the Union. Here, at a spot called "Pidgeon Creek Farm," near what became Gentryville in Spencer County, Lincoln's father built what was known on the frontier as a "half-faced camp"—a structure closed on three sides only, and open on the fourth save for a curtain of skins. In this rude shelter the family lived throughout that winter and indeed almost for twelve months, before a cabin could be constructed. In the autumn of 1818 an epidemic of illness, called the "milk sickness," came upon the settlement; it was thirty miles to the nearest doctor. Lincoln's mother, Nancy Hanks Lincoln, of whom we know very little, fell a victim to the sickness, and on October 5 she died. Abraham's older sister Sarah, who was only eleven, was left to manage the household throughout that winter and until, in the autumn of the following year, Lincoln's father married again. His second wife, Sally Bush Johnston, was a widow with three children. She was sensible, energetic and kind, and she soon made life a little easier for Thomas Lincoln's family. In particular she encouraged Abraham to make what use he could of the meagre opportunities that existed for schooling. He had a strong affection for her, and he often acknowledged his debt to her. She lived to see him President of the United States and to receive the news of his death with the patient fatalism of a very old woman.

Lincoln himself has told us something of what his life was like in those days.

"It was a wild region"—he wrote in 1859—"with many bears and other wild animals still in the woods. There I grew up. There were some schools, so called, but no qualification was ever required of a teacher beyond 'readin', writin', and cipherin'' to the rule of three. If a straggler supposed to understand Latin happened to sojourn in the neighborhood he was looked upon as a wizard. There was absolutely nothing to excite ambition for education. Of course, when I came of age I did not know much. Still, somehow, I could read, write and cipher to the rule of three, but that was all. I have not been to school since. The little advance I now have upon this store of education I have picked up from time to time under the pressure of necessity."

This lack of opportunity for schooling is a symbol of the life which was led on the frontier. Lincoln appears to have had five short sessions of schooling—two in Kentucky and three in Indiana—scattered over a period of five years, and in all they add up to less than a twelvemonth. He had to learn for himself. He read diligently, his stepmother says, and read every book he could lay his hands on. There were not many, but he seems to have been able to obtain *The Bible*, *Robinson Crusoe*, *Æsop's Fables*, *The Pilgrim's Progress*, Weems' *Life of Washington* and a *History of the United States*. And when these failed he turned to the Revised Statutes of Indiana, available at the house of the village constable.

But the day's work was not reading. It was wielding the axe, first put into his hands at eight years old; hewing the wood and drawing the water; planting the corn; catching fish and game. It was a hard life and not very healthy. There was one exciting and eye-opening adventure—a trip by flat boat down the Mississippi to New Orleans. Here, at the age of nineteen, he saw the first great city he had ever seen, and a community as cosmopolitan, as colourful, as squalid, as seething with life and commerce and conflict, as could well be imagined. He came back by steamboat, and there can be no doubt that the whole trip made a strong impression upon him.

After Kentucky and Indiana came, in March 1830, when Lincoln was twenty-one, the move into the third frontier state in which his life was spent—Illinois. In this state he lived until his election as President. Illinois had been admitted as a state of the Union—the twenty-first state—in 1818.

"Here"—says Lincoln—"they built a log cabin, into which they removed, and made sufficient of rails to fence ten acres of ground, fenced and broke the ground and raised a crop of sown corn upon it the same year. . . . In the autumn all hands were greatly afflicted with ague and fever, to which they had not been used, and by which they were greatly discouraged, so much so that they determined on leaving the county. They remained, however, through the succeeding winter, which was the winter of the very celebrated 'deep snow' of Illinois."

From this time begins that part of the life of Abraham Lincoln which is of greatest interest here. He was now twenty-one and, in accordance with the custom of the frontier, he left his father's cabin to take up life on his own account. It will be necessary to follow his succeeding years in some detail, but it is always to be remembered that they began and they continued in the lands of the frontier.

But the frontier influenced the life of Abraham Lincoln in ways which go far beyond the fact that he was born and lived in frontier states. It was the political problems of developing the frontier lands of the United States that produced the critical issues upon which the political career of Lincoln was founded. And this makes it necessary to record that the lands in which these problems were to arise were not solely those lands lying westward to the Mississippi ceded by Britain in 1783, and out of which Kentucky, Indiana and Illinois, the states of Lincoln's birth, boyhood and manhood, were established. There was first of all the "Louisiana Purchase" of 1803, six years before the birth of Lincoln. By the courageous act of President Jefferson, in his first term of office, the United States purchased from Napoleon I what was called Louisiana, an expanse of country as large as the United States itself at that time, and extending from the Gulf of Mexico, where it was no wider than the modern state of Louisiana, right up, roughly speaking,[2] to what is now the northern boundary of the United States. Within its confines have been established, in whole or in part, thirteen[3] states of the American Union. To this was added by 1819, when Lincoln was ten, Florida and a strip of land which joined the states of Mississippi and Alabama with the Gulf of Mexico —a long, complicated transaction with Spain, part conquest,

[2] In 1818 a part of the Louisiana Purchase was ceded to Britain in exchange for a part of Canada.

[3] Montana, North Dakota, South Dakota, Minnesota, Wyoming, Nebraska, Kansas, Iowa, Colorado, Missouri, Oklahoma, Arkansas, Louisiana.

part purchase. So it rested substantially through Lincoln's boyhood and young manhood, and then in the 1840's came a great burst of expansion which added to the United States all the land that lay between her western boundaries and the Pacific Ocean. There was the Texas annexation of 1845, the final acquisition, by treaty with Great Britain, of the Oregon country in 1846, and the Mexican cession of 1848. These were to provide problems in the years of Lincoln's manhood. But already in his boyhood there had been rung what Jefferson, then in his old age, called "a fire bell in the night." A crisis had arisen in the organisation of that part of the frontier called the Louisiana Purchase, because of a controversy of which we have said nothing so far, but which takes us back once more to consider Kentucky.

It was said that the second important thing about Kentucky, the state of Lincoln's birth, was that it was not one of the original thirteen states; it was a frontier state. The third important thing about Kentucky is that it was a slave state. But the importance lies not in any supposed influence that life in a slave state might have had on Lincoln's mind—it is doubtful if he ever saw a slave while he lived in Kentucky—but the fact that a state, not one of the original thirteen, should be a slave state. It leads us at once into the nature of the slave question in the United States.

When the American Union was inaugurated in 1789, all the original thirteen states except one—Massachusetts—recognised slavery. But the majority of the leaders at the Convention in Philadelphia which drew up the Constitution were opposed to slavery—men like Washington, John Adams, Jefferson and Madison, to name the first four Presidents of the United States. But it had been found that South Carolina and Georgia were unwilling to enter the Union unless slavery was permitted within their borders, and thus it came about that the Constitution of the United States recognised the existence of slavery—although the word itself is not used—and made certain concessions to the slave-holding states. There was, for example, a provision relating to the return of slaves who escaped. "No person held to service or labour in one state, under the laws thereof, escaping into another, shall, in consequence of any law or regulation therein, be discharged from such service or labour, but shall be delivered up on claim of the party to whom such service or labour may be due." There was, further, a provision in the Constitution forbidding Congress to pass legislation prohibiting the importation of slaves—the overseas slave trade—before 1808.

So far as the original states were concerned, it rested with them individually whether they abolished slavery or not. The Congress of the Union had no power under the Constitution of the United States to abolish slavery within the confines of the states. But what was its authority outside? A great controversy was to arise about the power of Congress to regulate slavery in "the Territories" as they were called, that is to say in those great tracts of land which had been acquired from the time of the War of Independence onwards. In so far as these lands were not made part of any state, they were subject to the jurisdiction of the United States, and the Constitution said that "the Congress shall have power to dispose of and make all needful rules and regulations respecting the Territories and other property belonging to the United States." In the course of time Congress divided up these lands into Territorial Governments, with a governor and judicature appointed by the President and with a legislature to assist in the making of the ordinances, but with the whole machine subordinate to the President and Congress of the United States. One by one these Territories or parts of them applied to be admitted into the Union as fully-fledged states and it was for Congress to decided whether they should be admitted. With few exceptions, all the states of the American Union, outside the original thirteen, passed through this stage of being a Territory with a Territorial Government.[4] The word "Territory" has therefore a specialised meaning in American history and we shall hear much of it later in this book. At this stage, however, the significant point to notice is that it was assumed in the early years of the Union that Congress had power, in the course of making rules for the Territories and in setting up Territorial Governments, to determine whether

---

[4] The exceptions were Kentucky itself (which went straight into statehood from being a part of Virginia), Vermont, Maine, Texas, California and West Virginia.

slavery should or should not be permitted in the Territories. This was an important power for it determined also whether these Territories, when they came to apply for admission as states, would apply for admission as free states or as slave states. And it had been exercised at the outset in an important direction which must be noted here.

In 1787, two years before the Constitution of the United States came into operation, an ordinance had been passed by the Congress of the Confederation, which had preceded the Union, to regulate a portion of the land ceded by Great Britain, known as the North-West Territory, the Territory which was later carved into the states of Michigan, Wisconsin, Illinois, Indiana and Ohio. Part of this ordinance of 1787 provided that there should be no slavery in the North-West Territory. The ordinance was re-enacted by Congress under the new Constitution in 1789, and thus at the outset of the Union one portion of the Territories was denied to slavery. The future of the rest of the Territories would rest with subsequent decisions of Congress.

In the early years of the Union the movement towards the abolition of slavery gained ground. In the Northern states, where slave labour was not much used, abolition was actually carried in some cases. In the Southern states, where cotton plantations existed, slave labour was relied upon principally, but there were those who hoped that as time went on slavery might gradually disappear there also. But in 1793 Eli Whitney invented the cotton gin, a simple machine, a sort of brush, for removing the seeds from cotton. This revolutionised the cotton industry. Even an unskilful slave could clean a thousand pounds of cotton of its seeds in one day, instead of five or six pounds as formerly. At once the Southern states became the great cotton field of the world. The industry developed enormously, and slavery, held to be essential to its efficient conduct, was thereafter the basis of prosperity and society in the Southern states. There could be no hope of its abolition there. But more important still, it became clear that in those portions of the Territories of the United States where cotton could be grown, slavery would be considered essential. There would be a demand to open up to slavery some portions at any rate of the Territories. Thus there developed a conflict of view, based upon an economic division, between the Northern and Southern states in the American Union about the institution of slavery. More particularly that conflict would show itself concerning the *extension* of slavery. It became a matter of importance to each section whether new states admitted by Congress to the Union should be admitted as slave states or free states. Though in the lower house of Congress, the House of Representatives, each state was represented according to population, in the Senate each state was represented by two members irrespective of its population, and the balance of slave states and free states was anxiously watched there. The custom grew up, in order to preserve some sort of balance, of admitting, alternately or in pairs, slave states and free states. Upon this balance in the Senate, more than anywhere else, depended the decision whether Congress would extend slavery into the Territories or not.

In 1809, the year of Lincoln's birth, there were seventeen states in the Union. Of these seventeen, eight were slave states and nine were free. It is interesting to see how these totals were made up. Let us look first at the original thirteen. Seven of these states had abolished slavery within their borders— New Hampshire, Massachusetts, New York, Pennsylvania, Connecticut, Rhode Island and New Jersey. The remaining six lying to the south of them still preserved slavery— Maryland, Virginia, Delaware, North Carolina, South Carolina and Georgia. Of the four states added to the original thirteen, Vermont, admitted in 1791, belonged to the extreme North and came in as a free state; Kentucky, the state of Lincoln's birth, admitted in 1792, lay in the South to the west of Virginia, of which it had once been part, and it was accordingly a slave state. Tennessee, to the south of Kentucky, admitted in 1796, was another slave state; and in 1802 the turn of the free states came with the admission of Ohio, carved out of the North-West Territory and therefore required to be free by the North-West Territory Ordinance of 1787, already mentioned.

The boundary which divided the free states of the North from the slave states of the South, at the date of Lincoln's birth, is sometimes called "the Mason and Dixon line." It was drawn originally between 1763 and 1767 by two English surveyors named Mason and Dixon, to divide Pennsylvania from Delaware and Maryland, and it ran along the line of latitude 39° 43′ 26.3″. At the establishment of the Union the Mason and Dixon line had come in practice to represent the boundary between the farming and commercial states of the North and the plantation states of the South. With the abolition of slavery in the seven Northern states of the original thirteen, the Mason and Dixon line came to mark the boundary of free states from slave states. But to these original seven free states there had been added the North-West Territory protected against slavery by the Ordinance of 1787. The boundaries of free soil and slave soil were thus extended. It came to be the custom to speak of an extended Mason and Dixon line, which included not only the original line, separating Pennsylvania from Maryland and Delaware, but also a line formed by the Ohio river from its intersection with the Pennsylvania boundary to its junction with the Mississippi.

Such was the fundamental compromise about slavery in the United States when Abraham Lincoln was born. The powers given to Congress were to be exercised on this understanding. The Constitution itself gave no sanctity to the Mason and Dixon line; it was purely a convention or understanding with no legal safeguards, but it was based upon certain economic and social divisions among the states which made it appear a practical compromise. And so it worked for the first eleven years of Lincoln's life. In 1812, when Lincoln was three years old, Louisiana was admitted to the Union, the first state to be erected from the Louisiana Purchase. Slavery had been established there under the French régime, and Louisiana was naturally admitted as a slave state. This made the numbers of free states and slave states equal —nine each. In 1816 Indiana, lying within the Territory governed by the North-West Territory Ordinance, and thereby denied to slavery, was admitted as a free state; it was followed in 1817 by Mississippi far in the South, and a slave state. Then followed Illinois in 1818, lying to the west of Indiana, another state from the North-West Territory and therefore free; and in 1819 Alabama in the South, lying between Georgia and Mississippi, and a slave state. Thus it stood in

1819, when Lincoln was in his eleventh year, eleven free states and eleven slave states—half slave and half free.

Half slave and half free. Almost forty years later, on June 16, 1858, Abraham Lincoln declared: "I believe this government cannot endure, permanently half slave and half free." It was a solemn and awful prediction. In 1819, however, there occurred an event which, to those who could remember it in 1858—and Lincoln was one—must have been full of warning. At the very moment when the states were equally divided, a proposal was made which upset the equilibrium. The people of the Territory of Upper Louisiana, lying to the north of the state of Louisiana, and part, of course, of the Louisiana Purchase, decided to claim admission to the Union as the state of Missouri. Congress, in organising Territorial Governments in the lands of the Louisiana Purchase, had taken no action to disturb or remove slavery there. It had been permitted under French and Spanish law; several thousand slave-holders had settled in the Territory which now claimed admission to the Union as a state, and it was natural that they should claim admission as a slave state. Here, for the first time, the problem of developing the lands of the Louisiana Purchase became acute. The Mason and Dixon line so far had been extended along the course of the Ohio river to its junction with the Mississippi, and it had marked the northern boundary of slavery in the Territories ceded by Britain. But was it to stop there? Or should it be continued across the lands of the Louisiana Purchase? The proposed new state of Missouri would prevent this extension, for its boundaries lay almost entirely to the north of such an extended Mason and Dixon line. It seemed to be the spearhead of an encircling movement by the slave states to prevent the further advance westward of free states. The Northern states saw in this an attempt to extend slavery throughout the great new Western lands and to destroy the old division based upon the Mason and Dixon line. When the bill to admit Missouri as a slave state was introduced into Congress, James Tallmadge, of New York, carried an amendment in the House of Representatives, prohibiting the further introduction of slaves into Missouri and providing that all children subsequently born there of slave parents should be free at the age of twenty-five. The Southern states were angered by this action and the amendment was defeated in the Senate. The controversy that occurred upon this issue was "the fire bell in the night" which alarmed Thomas Jefferson.

The outcome was a compromise, the Missouri Compromise, adopted and enacted by Congress in 1820. It was agreed that Missouri should be admitted as a slave state. At the same time it was agreed that Maine, which had detached itself from Massachusetts, and lay in the extreme North, should also be admitted. It was, of course, a free state, and the totals were twelve each. But the compromise went further. Although Missouri was to be a slave state, slavery was to be prohibited elsewhere in the Territories of the Louisiana Purchase to the north of latitude 36° 30', the latitude of the southern boundary of Missouri, and roughly the southern boundary of Kentucky and Virginia also. This was considered a fair compromise. The South obtained its immediate object—that Missouri should enter as a slave state. It could anticipate the admission also, as slave states, of Florida (formed from the land acquired in 1819 from Spain) and Arkansas, lying between the states of Louisiana and Missouri. The North secured that the greater expanse of the unsettled lands in the Louisiana Purchase should be forbidden to slavery. The Mason and Dixon line was now extended to run from the junction of the Ohio and Mississippi along the eastern, northern and western borders of Missouri and thence along the line of latitude 36° 30' to the west. This brought the southern boundary of free soil to a point considerably lower than that of the Mason and Dixon line as it stood before the compromise.

But two other important issues appeared to be settled by the Missouri Compromise. It appeared to assume that Congress could impose conditions upon the admission of new states. This had, in fact, been assumed in the case of states carved out of the North-West Territory and of the Louisiana Purchase. It was challenged in 1819 by those who objected to the Tallmadge amendment. But the enacting of the Missouri Compromise assumed the existence of such a power. The second assumption in the Compromise was that Congress had power to determine whether or not slavery could be introduced into the Territories. The North-West Ordinance of 1787 had been founded upon this principle. The legislation of 1820 proceeded upon the assumption that Congress was entitled to prohibit slavery in the Territories by virtue of the power conferred upon it in the Constitution, and already referred to, of regulating the Territories. These two great assumptions were one day to be violently challenged and were to exercise a critical influence upon the career of Abraham Lincoln.

An English reader will be inclined to ask: What is surprising about these assumptions? Why should it not be assumed that the Congress of the United States was able to prohibit slavery or to impose conditions upon new states when it admitted them into the Union, and indeed to pass any legislative enactment which it thought fit, just as the Parliament of the United Kingdom could do? It is well to stress at once that the powers of the Congress of the United States and of the Parliament of the United Kingdom are quite different. There is no legal limit to the law-making power of Parliament in the United Kingdom. But in the United States the powers of Congress are limited by the Constitution, and it cannot therefore be assumed that all acts of Congress are valid. The powers of government in America are divided under the Constitution between a general government for the Union and distinct governments for each of the states. Laws for the Union, in accordance with powers conferred by the Constitution, could be made by the Congress—the House of Representatives and the Senate—of the United States, subject to the consent of the President, whose refusal of assent could be overridden by a two-thirds majority in each house. Laws for the states were made by state legislatures, each composed of two houses also, usually called a House of Representatives and a Senate, and subject to the consent of a governor. There was a dual system of government in America, and not least powerful were the governments of the states.

So we come back to Kentucky, the state of Lincoln's birth, and to the significant fact that it was not only a frontier state, but also a slave state. And the significance of its slavery lies, not in any influence it might be imagined to have had upon

Lincoln's early years, but rather in the fact that Kentucky was a symbol. It was the first of the frontier states to be admitted, and it was admitted as a slave state. It is the symbol of that link between the development of the frontier and the extension of slavery, of the problem whether slavery should follow the frontier or not, which is the fundamental problem of politics in the lifetime of Abraham Lincoln.

Chapter 2

State Politics

"Years trying how to learn to handle men,
  Which can be done, if you've got heart enough,
  And how to deal with women or a woman
  And that's about the hardest task I know."
STEPHEN VINCENT BENÉT: *John Brown's Body*.

IN MARCH 1831, after the winter of the "deep snow" in Illinois, Abraham Lincoln left his father's cabin to start life on his own account. His family had settled in Illinois first near Decatur, but soon moved off again to Coles County, and his ways and theirs now parted. Once more he took a flat boat down the river to New Orleans, this time for a trader and speculator named Denton Offut, and when he returned he contracted to act as clerk for Offut in charge of his store and mill at a little place of about a hundred souls called New Salem, then in Sangamon County. Andrew Jackson was now President of the United States—the seventh President—and it was in his time and under his strong influence that the Democratic party came to be known by that name (they had first called themselves Republicans and then Republican-Democrats) and to partake of that nature. For Jackson was a frontiersman. He came from the state of Tennessee and he was the first President from the frontier; all his predecessors had come from the original thirteen states. He brought the rude, direct methods of the frontier to the White House; he brought the West into the sphere which had formerly known only North and South.

Illinois was strong for Jackson; it was an overwhelmingly Democratic state. True, the opposition party, now organised under the name of the Whigs and led in the country by Henry Clay, had some support in the state, but it was small. Nor is this surprising. What state more likely to support the frontiersman in the White House than the frontier state of Illinois?

And what man more likely to support the frontiersman than Abraham Lincoln? But it was not so. Lincoln was a Whig, a follower of Henry Clay. This is a surprising fact and it is not easy to find any adequate explanation. No biographer of Lincoln appears to have examined the question thoroughly. It may be that Lincoln was influenced by the powerful figure of Henry Clay and his advocacy of a national bank for the United States, of high tariffs, and of a policy of "internal improvements" or development works, such as railways, roads and canals. It may be that his earliest friends in New Salem had Whig leanings. Perhaps those Southern influences which were strong in Kentucky and southern Indiana had favoured the Whigs—for the Whig party at this time had a distinguished support in the South—and had had an effect upon Lincoln's political opinions. However it may be, he announced himself in March 1832 as a candidate for election to the House of Representatives of Illinois, and he ran as a Whig.

So Lincoln was "a Clay man in a Jacksonian family and a Democratic state. His politics came by independent reasoning, not by inheritance or inertia."[1] And one is inclined to follow the example of Lincoln's "official" biographers, Nicolay and Hay, who were his secretaries when he became President, and remark upon the moral courage and the absence of the shuffling politician's fair-weather policy which led Lincoln "in his obscure and penniless youth, at the very beginning of his career, when he was not embarrassed by antecedents or family connections, and when, in fact, what little social influence he knew would have led him the other way . . . to take his stand with the party which was doomed to long continued defeat in Illinois."

At the same time we have to remember that there was some Whig support in the state, and in particular in Sangamon County, which was, after all, the district for which Lincoln would stand if he wished to get into the state legislature. His prospects as a Whig were not hopeless in his county, but if he considered the prospects of power in the state or of election to Congress, then the Whig party was likely to be the party of opposition not of power.

[1] J. G. Randall, *Lincoln, the President,* p. 8.

Whatever the influences were which made Lincoln choose the Whigs, the fact that he did choose them proved of great consequence. Had he chosen the Democrats, his whole political career might have been different. When, as time passed, the Democratic party found itself more and more divided upon the issue of slavery, and when it came to base itself more on the South and to lose the West, Lincoln would have reached a great crisis of decision in his life. Would he have left his party? And what future would he have had in that event? Or would he have influenced his party and been influenced by them and remained with them? These speculations are relatively fruitless. But it is worth raising these questions if only to stress the fact that there would have been nothing surprising in Lincoln's beginning his political career as a Democrat and coming later to hold views which led him to oppose the Democratic party. Many Democrats in Lincoln's time had that experience. But if it had happened to Lincoln, the history of the United States might have been different.

When the election for the Illinois legislature occurred in August 1832, Lincoln was defeated. Sangamon County was entitled to return four members. There were twelve candidates. Lincoln came seventh, and it is interesting to record that in his own locality or "precinct" (as it is called in American electoral organisation) of New Salem, he obtained 277 out of the 280 votes cast. Not all the successful candidates were Democrats, one at least, John T. Stuart, being a Whig. From Lincoln's point of view it was not a bad result for a young man of twenty-three, unknown outside his small village and with no advantages of wealth and position. What is significant is that this almost unknown young man should have put himself forward as a candidate.

Already it was quite clear that Lincoln liked politics and that he wanted to get into political life. He was ambitious. It is important to recognise this fact right at the start. Lincoln's career is not that of a man who finds himself reluctantly pushed forward into public life while all the time his heart longs for the quiet and peace of home and private affairs. Lincoln wanted to engage in politics. He put himself forward as a candidate in 1832, and this action was perfectly in accordance with his character. There was, of course, more to it than mere ambition. He was popular, honest, clear-headed, and he wanted to do something for the people of his state. But without ambition his political career would not have occurred. For the time being, however, it was postponed. His defeat in 1832 had one unique characteristic. It was the only occasion, as he remembered throughout his life with great pride, that he was ever beaten on a direct vote of the people.

For the moment Lincoln's fortunes were very low. His job as a clerk in Offut's store had ceased because the store had failed. He had had a short spell as a soldier earlier in 1832. Black Hawk, an Indian chief, had united some tribes under his command and was threatening to invade the northern part of Illinois and reoccupy their old homes there. The Governor of Illinois called for volunteers to march against Black Hawk. Lincoln had joined and been elected captain of his company There proved to be no serious fighting; he was mustered out in June and reached home in time for his election campaign. After this came a period as joint owner with a man called Berry of a store, bought on credit. But Berry was worthless, and after a series of unsuccessful attempts to rid themselves of the burden of the property, Lincoln found himself finally saddled with the debts. It took him seventeen years to pay them off. They were a very great burden on his early years of struggle to make a living. But these years of industry and economy gave him a reputation for honesty which was of great value.

Out of this failure he was rescued to some extent by being appointed postmaster of New Salem. He held this position for three years, from May 7, 1833, to May 30, 1836, when New Salem had declined so considerably in population that the office was removed to the neighbouring village of Petersburg. This appointment is surprising. Postmasterships in the United States at that time—and still—were appointments in the gift of the President of the United States, and they would normally go to supporters of the President's party; they were a recognised way of rewarding party service and supporting party organisation. Now President Jackson was a Democrat; but Lincoln was a Whig. Why should he obtain the post? There is no explanation available. He said himself he supposed the office was "too insignificant to make his politics an objection." No Democrat wanted so small a job. It has been suggested that he had acted for some time as deputy to the former postmaster, and that when the office fell vacant, he was the natural successor. At any rate, it is interesting to notice that this, the first office under the United States which Lincoln held, was given him by the Democrats. He held one other only, the Presidency, and that he took away from them.

There was not much money in a postmastership for a man with debts to pay off, and it was, in American politics, not a job with a certain future. Its great advantage for Abraham was that it gave him a chance to read the newspapers as they arrived and to talk to folks about politics. To it Lincoln was able to add, in the summer of 1833, the post of deputy-surveyor for the county. In this way, as he said, he "procured bread, and kept soul and body together." And on this precarious foundation in 1834 he once again offered himself as a candidate for election to the House of Representatives of Illinois.[2] This time he was elected, coming top of the poll. The next two successful candidates were Democrats, and the fourth was John T. Stuart, the Whig. It was the start of Lincoln's political career. He was to be re-elected three times, and thus had a period of eight years as a member of the state legislature.

It was a remarkable success, this first election in 1834. To come out at the head of the poll as a Whig, to be in advance of two older and established Democrats, one of whom had already served a term in the House, and to out-distance the most prominent young man in the district, John T. Stuart, who had been elected to the House in 1832 when Lincoln had failed and who was regarded as the most likely Whig candidate for election to the House of Representatives of the United States in the near future—these were great achievements. They give some indication of Lincoln's personal position in New Salem and in the surrounding country. He knew people; he liked to talk to them. He was friendly and humorous and poor and honest. He did not drink or smoke;

[2] The term of office of the House was fixed at two years; general elections were held on the first Monday in August in the even-numbered years.

he had great physical strength, and indeed enjoyed a fantastic reputation as a weight-lifter. He could use his fists if need be, but appears to have intervened reluctantly and on the side of justice. All these qualities had contributed to his personal popularity and success, and were to maintain him as a member of the state legislature for eight years.

During this period of eight years three events occurred in the life of Abraham Lincoln which were of lasting importance and which, therefore, require some discussion. The first was his discovery of a permanent means of livelihood. On March 1, 1837, the name of Abraham Lincoln was formally enrolled as an attorney, licensed to practice law in all the courts of Illinois. For some years he had wished to become a lawyer. In 1832, when defeated at the election for the state legislature, he tells us that he "thought of learning the blacksmith's trade, thought of trying to study law, rather thought he could not succeed at that without a better education." He had tried to improve his education by reading when he could. But his real opportunity to take up the law came when he was elected to the state legislature in 1834. For the other successful Whig candidate, John T. Stuart, was a lawyer in practice at Springfield, Illinois. Stuart had become friendly with Lincoln. He too had been a volunteer in the Black Hawk War, and they were both Whigs. Stuart encouraged Lincoln to study law. Lincoln himself tells us that "after the election, he borrowed books of Stuart, took them home with him, and went at it in good earnest. He studied with nobody. . . ." In September 1836 he applied for and was granted a law license by the Supreme Court of Illinois, and he was formally enrolled in the following spring. On April 12, 1837, Lincoln arranged to become the law partner of Stuart, and three days later he moved from New Salem to Springfield to begin the practice of the law.

So at last Lincoln had found a means of livelihood, and it was congenial. The partnership with Stuart lasted until 1841, when it was dissolved because Stuart, who had been elected to the House of Representatives in Washington in 1839, had not been able to devote more than a fraction of his time to the legal practice. Lincoln then formed a partnership with Judge Stephen T. Logan, whom he had known in his practice on circuit, and who had retired from the bench in 1837 to return to practice. Logan was primarily interested in the law, and indeed stood at the head of the Illinois bar, whereas Stuart had devoted himself largely to politics, and knew and cared little about the law. The change of partnership was of benefit to Lincoln. Although it did not last for more than three and a half years, it gave Lincoln his most thorough and constructive training in the law; it made him a good, all-round, well-founded lawyer. And with it he obtained a standing in the community, security and a serious profession. In 1844 Logan wished to take his son into partnership and Lincoln felt able to start his own firm. So he formed a partnership with William H. Herndon in the autumn of 1844. It was a curious choice, for Herndon was not admitted to the bar until December 1844, and he was young and inexperienced. Yet it proved a perfect combination and, as Herndon said: "Our partnership was never legally dissolved until the night of his assassination."

Thus by stages Lincoln became established in the profession which he was to follow for the rest of his life, and which, with politics, absorbed the greater part of his energies. He had been admitted, on December 3, 1839, to practise before the courts of the United States, as well as those of the state of Illinois. And indeed the practice of the law in the frontier states was hard work. Most of the time was spent on circuit, riding round with the judge from township to township; sharing the primitive accommodation available and taking the weather and the business as it came. But Lincoln seems to have been at home in it. He liked the talk and the argument; he got a chance to explain on circuit what he had been doing in the legislature; to talk politics and to gain experience.

When Lincoln began his practice of the law, he moved from New Salem to Springfield; his partnership with Stuart made that move necessary. This change to Springfield was the second important event which must be noticed. There is an odd coincidence about it, of no significance beyond its oddity. Lincoln entered Springfield on April 15, 1837. He was then twenty-eight. He had exactly twenty-eight more years to live to the very day, for it was on April 15, 1865, that he died. But the move to Springfield has greater significance. It was the change from a village to a large town, from a settlement with twenty houses and one hundred people to a "city" of about two thousand inhabitants. Not that the amenities of that city would seem good by the standards of the cities of the Eastern states of America at that time. There were no public buildings and no paved streets; there was no railway. But for Lincoln there was a wider society. He lodged with Joshua Speed, a storekeeper, free of charge. Speed had a double bed upstairs, and the two men slept in it, according to the custom of a frontier city. In the room at the back of the store, round a large fireplace, Speed and his friends talked at night. Lincoln formed a close friendship with Speed. There too he met William Herndon, then Speed's clerk and Lincoln's future partner and his political manager and adviser. Most interesting of all, there was Stephen A. Douglas, later to become Lincoln's great political antagonist in public debate. Douglas was a Democrat, and already a rising politician in the Illinois legislature, and in these discussions in Speed's kitchen Lincoln and he were already opposed to each other.

Springfield was important also because it became the capital of the state of Illinois. When Lincoln first came to the state and when he was first a member of the legislature, the capital was situated at Vandalia, a village of about eight hundred people, and it was thither that Lincoln journeyed from New Salem to attend the sittings of the legislature, riding there and back on horseback. The decision to make the move to Springfield was taken in 1837. The representatives of Sangamon County were strongly in support of the proposal because Springfield was in their county, and Lincoln appears to have had a large share in carrying the measure through the legislature. The move was actually made in 1839, and thereafter Lincoln shared the advantages, in law and politics, which residence in the capital gave.

Lincoln's residence in Springfield brought him into "fashionable society" as it was conceived in Springfield in those days. And for the first time he met women of some education and social sense. He appears to have enjoyed the experience, although to outsiders he is said to have looked "like a rustic on his first visit to the circus." At Springfield, in 1839, he met Mary Todd; and towards the end of 1840 he became engaged to her. But at the beginning of the next year, possibly on January 1, 1841, he seems to have broken off, or to have attempted to break off, his engagement. He was passing, at this time, through a period of acute depression, a feature of his make-up which had shown itself in recent years and which he never wholly overcame. On November 4, 1842, almost two years later, they were married. It is his marriage to Mary Todd that makes the third important event of these years.

Of this marriage much has been written, with great violence sometimes, by partisans of either side. Whether it was a happy marriage is an open question. Upon whom the greater share of blame must rest it is difficult to say. Lincoln was not an easy man to live with—melancholy, abstracted and awkward. Though he appears to have liked the company of women, his relations with them appear to have given him more misery than happiness. The story that already, while at New Salem, he had fallen in love with Ann Rutledge, who died in August 1835, and that her death cast him into a prolonged depression, is now thought to have little foundation.[8] In 1836, however, he had proposed marriage to Mary Owens, a year older than himself and rather stout. He described her to a friend as "a fair match for Falstaff." It was a curious, half-hearted, mismanaged proposal, and it made him introspective and unhappy. When Joshua Speed first saw him at Springfield in 1837, he said: "I never saw so gloomy and melancholy a face in my life." From Springfield Lincoln wrote to Mary Owens to explain to her why she should not marry him. And finally she broke the affair off. His relations with Mary Todd during their courtship were similarly indecisive and miserable.

Mary Todd Lincoln was often unhappy. She appears to have had an excitable and violent temperament; she lost her temper and was jealous. Lincoln did little to placate her at these times. Instead he sat silent and sad, or got up and went off to his office. The neighbours told stories of her ungovernable temper and of Lincoln's occasional counter-attacks. One

---

[8] The evidence is critically examined in Randall, *Lincoln, the President*, vol. 2, Appendix.

neighbour summed it up like this: "Lincoln and his wife got along tolerably well, unless Mrs. L. got the devil in her; Lincoln . . . would pick up one of his children and walk off —would laugh at her—pay no earthly attention to her when in that wild furious condition." Against all this it is fair to record that Mary Lincoln had qualities which complemented those of Abraham Lincoln; she shared his ambitions in politics; she was as eager for his advancement as he was. There are preserved some letters they wrote to each other in their married life which are tender, true and at the same time practical and sensible. No other woman took her place in his affections. Yet when all is said, it is clear that Lincoln's marriage did not make him happy. But would he have been happier with any other woman? There is some wisdom in this simple and pathetic little sentence which Mary Owens (then Mrs. Vineyard) wrote after Lincoln's death: "I thought Mr. Lincoln was deficient in those little links which make up the great chain of woman's happiness." It seems clear that Lincoln had not the temperament of a man who could take the trouble to make an unhappy woman happy.

While these three important events occurred—the law partnership in 1837, the removal to Springfield at the same time and his marriage in 1842—Lincoln was serving his four terms of two years each as a member of the Illinois state legislature. His work in the legislature was in general undistinguished. He belonged to the minority party, the Whigs, and therefore opportunities were denied to him which he could have had as a Democrat. He did his share in supporting projects for "internal improvements," as they were called at the time—the policy of building roads, railways and canals to develop the state—and he had his share of responsibility for the failure of a good deal of this policy, which was, in fact, overdone. In this Lincoln was pretty much like the other politicians of his state. His share in arranging the transfer of the state capital from Vandalia to Springfield has already been mentioned. This was a piece of local patriotism, typical of the sort of issues which were the stuff of politics in the frontier states. For the rest he was evidently popular and influential in his party, for they nominated him in 1838 and 1840 as their candidate for the speakership of the House of Representatives, a post occupied by a party leader in an American legislature and not that of impartial chairman as in the House of Commons. He was not elected, of course, as his party were in a minority. But his nomination meant that he was the leading Whig in the House.

There was one issue with which Lincoln was concerned at this time which deserves special mention because it falls into a different category. Not that what he did altered the course of events in his state at the time, but the attitude he took has a significance for the future. The issue arose out of the slavery question. On January 1, 1831, William Lloyd Garrison had produced the first number of *The Liberator*, an anti-slavery newspaper. A year later he founded the New England Anti-Slavery Society, the first society in America to advocate and work for the immediate abolition of slavery. From this time the abolition movement gained in strength and the formation of Abolition Societies spread among the states. The activities of the Abolitionists aroused the most violent passions. They themselves spoke in unreserved language against slavery and slave-holders. Not only so, but they attacked those who believed that slavery would disappear gradually or should be removed by slow stages. They favoured immediate and total abolition. "No union with slave-holders" was to be their watchword. They were prepared to sacrifice the American Union for abolition if that were necessary.

Illinois, lying to the north of the Mason and Dixon line, and carved out of the North-West Territory, had been admitted into the Union as a free state, and, in spite of an attempt in 1822–3 to change the situation, it remained free. But many of the people of Illinois had come from Kentucky and favoured slavery. The great majority were opposed, at any rate, to Abolitionism. Indeed in November 1838, at Alton, Illinois, an Abolitionist, Elijah Lovejoy, was killed by a mob for persisting in printing an anti-slavery newspaper. In March 1837, however, the legislature of Illinois had passed a series of resolutions "highly disapproving abolition societies" and holding that "the right of property in slaves is secured to the slave-holding states by the Federal Constitution." There were only six dissentients to the resolutions; two of them caused to be entered upon the Journals of the House a protest against the resolutions, and one of these two was Abraham Lincoln.

The protest was not extreme. It was phrased reasonably and it took up a moderate position. It ran: "They believe that the institution of slavery is founded on both injustice and bad policy, but that the promulgation of abolition doctrines tends rather to increase than abate its evils." There followed a recognition of the fact that, while under the Constitution Congress had no power to interfere with slavery inside the different states, yet, so far as the District of Columbia was concerned—the territory in which the Federal capital of Washington was situated and for which Congress had power to legislate directly—Congress did have power to abolish slavery, although that power ought not to be exercised, except at the request of the people of the District.

Lincoln himself, when a Congressman, was to propose some definite action towards the removal of slavery from the District of Columbia, and his views at this time have therefore an additional interest. But what is most significant here is the moderation of his views. He sees clearly and he says boldly that the institution of slavery is wrong. On the moral issue he is uncompromising. But he sees as clearly that the means to be adopted must be carefully chosen; that abolitionism and other forms of extremism make matters worse. On the political issue he is ready to compromise. This was the way of Lincoln's mind in his public life. Its earliest manifestation here deserves to be recorded and pondered.

Lincoln's eight years of service in the state legislature of Illinois came to an end in 1842, when he was thirty-three. He had intimated to his party when he was elected in 1840 that he would not stand again. The main reason for this appears to have been his desire to be elected to the Congress of the United States. His partner, Stuart, had served two terms in Congress, and Lincoln's ambitions were doubtless stimulated by his example. In 1840, also, a Whig had been elected to the Presidency, William Henry Harrison, and it looked as if the fortunes of the Whig party in the national government were to revive. But Lincoln's hopes were dashed when Harrison died a month after his inauguration and his successor, the Vice-President John Tyler, came more and

more under the control of the Democrats. In 1844 another
Democrat, James K. Polk, was elected to the Presidency, defeating Henry Clay, the Whig candidate. Lincoln took part
in both campaigns, 1840 and 1844, speaking in his state on
behalf of the Whig candidates, and in 1844 visting his old
friends at Gentryville in Indiana in the course of the campaign.

In the campaigns of 1840 and 1844 Lincoln was nominated
as an "elector" for the Presidency by the Whig party in his
state. This was a nominal office and little more than an
honour. It should be explained, perhaps, that under the Constitution of the United States the President is not directly
elected by the people. He is elected by what are called colleges of electors, chosen in each state by such means as the
legislature of that state determines. At this time most states
had provided that the electors should be chosen by the people
of the states, though South Carolina, for example, followed
the method of choosing the electors by the state legislature.
At a presidential election, therefore, the first task was to
choose the colleges of electors, and thereafter these colleges
of electors would choose a President. The practice soon arose
of the parties putting up their own list of candidates for the
posts of electors, each candidate being pledged to support
the party's candidate for the Presidency. The electors were
not expected to exercise their discretion. They were supposed
to register their party's will. So in Illinois Abraham Lincoln
was nominated as one of the Whig party's candidates for the
office of Presidential elector and his name figured on the
"ticket" which that party issued to its supporters and which
contained the names of all its candidates for the electoral
college of Illinois. It illustrates his place in the party organisation of the Whigs and it shows that although he had been
the leader of his group in the legislature, he was not yet
one of the powerful party leaders in his state.

Indeed it was not until 1846 that he was at last nominated
by his party for election to Congress. He won his election in
August 1846 as a member of the House of Representatives
in the Thirtieth Congress of the United States. He carried
the seat by 6,340 votes to 4,829 cast for his Democratic opponent—the largest majority by which the district had ever

been carried. Stephen A. Douglas, who had been a Congressman since 1842, having been re-elected in 1844, was successful once more in 1846, but soon afterwards the Illinois state legislature elected him to the Senate of the United States. Thus he and Lincoln did not face each other in Congress. Their conflicts were to be outside.

Lincoln's years in state politics are rather dull to read of now. There was not much in them to distinguish him from other politicians of his state, many of them lawyers like him. But it is possible to detect in his work at this time two characteristics which are fundamental to the understanding of his political life. They have been stressed already and they need therefore no more than a mention here. He wanted to succeed in politics: his election to Congress is the last of many illustrations of this. Lincoln had to persist and to negotiate and to manœuvre in order to obtain his election; and he was prepared to do it. He planned slowly; he was reflective and reserved; but he pressed towards his object. Nevertheless, with this ambition went a feeling for moderation and compromise in political action. His association with the extreme remedy of civil war at a great crisis in the history of his country has led people to think of him as a great prophet of revolution. Lincoln was a moderate man. His political actions can only be understood if that fact is grasped. The protest against the resolutions of 1837 in the Illinois legislature was the symbol of this fact in this first period of his career.

Chapter 3

Congressman

"The small-town lawyer, the crude small-time
   politician,
State character, but comparative failure at forty,
In spite of ambition enough for twenty Caesars."
STEPHEN VINCENT BENÉT: *John Brown's Body*.

THE TWO QUALITIES of ambition and moderation already noted marked Lincoln's career as a Congressman[1] also. Not that there was much scope for ambition in his single term of office. The House of Representatives was and is not organised to give new members much chance. A Congressman's term was two years only, in contrast with the six-year term of a Senator; but even these two years were greatly curtailed. A Congressman elected, as Lincoln was, in August 1846 did not take office until March of the following year, and did not actually take his seat and begin his legislative business until the following December. By that time there was less than a year to go before the next Congressional elections, so that members, although their term of office did not expire till March 1849, were preoccupied through a good part of the year 1848 with election prospects. This arrangement of the business of Congress, which lasted until 1933, meant that a very small part of the two-years term could be devoted to the serious business of legislation, and only a tiny fraction of the time was not overshadowed by approaching elections. The House of Representatives therefore was not the chamber which the leading politicians chose to enter. They preferred the longer term and the smaller size of the Senate—at this time the House of Representatives numbered something over

[1] It is usual to speak of a member of the House of Representatives alone as a Congressman, although strictly Congress is composed of both Senate and House, and "Congressman" should cover both.

two hundred members; the Senate in 1848 numbered sixty, two from each of the thirty states which, by that time, formed the Union. Stephen A. Douglas had naturally sought election as a Senator from Illinois and had achieved it in 1846 after two terms in the House. The man of ambition would hope to be promoted.

When Lincoln took his seat in Congress—the only Whig from Illinois—the burning issue of the time in national politics was the Mexican War. The issues were complicated, but the results of the war were to affect Lincoln's career. Texas had seceded from Mexico in 1836, largely as a result of the action of American settlers who had immigrated into the country from the Southern states, bringing their slaves with them. When it established itself as an independent republic, slavery was recognised in its constitution. After many years of negotiation, Texas was at last annexed by the United States in 1845, on the initiative of the Whig President Tyler, and with the consent of both Houses of Congress, and it became at once a state of the Union. It was a step viewed by some of the states of the Union with misgiving, and it had been opposed and rejected in the Senate when first put forward by Tyler in 1844. When annexation was carried out, the terms of the Missouri Compromise were applied to the new state— that is to say, slavery was not permitted above the line 36° 30′ north latitude.

But Texas was only a beginning. President Polk, a Democrat, who succeeded Tyler, had further designs for the United States, and he was supported in these by many leaders of the Southern states who for long had coveted the territories of Mexico, into which the Southern system of plantations and slavery might be extended. There was a dispute with Mexico about the boundary of Texas. The Rio Grande was claimed as the boundary by the United States; Mexico denied it. President Polk ordered General Zachary Taylor to march his troops up to the line of the Rio Grande and to occupy a position commanding the Mexican garrison there, encamped at the town of Matamoras on the opposite side of the river. The Mexican commander demanded that Taylor should retire, and, when he refused, crossed the river and ambushed some American dragoons on April 23, 1846. This, said President Polk, was an act of invasion. "Mexico," he said, in a message to Congress on May 11, 1846, "has passed the boundary of the United States, . . . and shed American blood on American soil. War exists, and exists by the act of Mexico itself." The course of the war need not be treated here. Mexico was defeated, and on February 2, 1848, during Lincoln's first session as a Congressman, a treaty was concluded between the United States and Mexico, at Guadalupe Hidalgo, by which Mexico ceded to the United States Texas with the Rio Grande boundary; New Mexico including Arizona; and Upper California—an extent of country in which are included today the states of Arizona, California, Nevada, Utah, and parts of Colorado, Wyoming and New Mexico.

By the annexation of Texas, the conquest of Mexico and by a treaty with Britain in 1846 over the Oregon country, the United States extended itself practically to its present-day limits. It remained only to complete the present southwestern boundary by the "Gadsden Purchase" from Mexico in 1853.

The Mexican War gave plenty of scope for controversy. It was popular in the states of the Mississippi valley and on the frontier; the original thirteen states were not so enthusiastic though South Carolina and Georgia favoured it; the abolitionists and the anti-slavery men were whole-heartedly against it. Wise Southern leaders like John C. Calhoun saw that more land meant more trouble because it upset the balance between the Northern and free states on the one hand and the Southern and slave states on the other, and would revive the dangerous question of slavery in the Territories. And indeed the most critical issues arose, not over the war itself, but over the development of the Territories it brought.

But the manner of bringing on the war aroused its own controversy, and the Whigs did not lose their opportunity to criticise President Polk. Lincoln's first venture as a Congressman was to offer a series of resolutions in the House of Representatives asking the President whether the spot upon which American blood was first spilled in the war with Mexico was United States or Mexican territory. The resolutions were set out in the form of eight questions propounded to the President, and they were designed to discredit the

President's assertion that Mexico had invaded the United States. These resolutions were proposed on December 22, 1847, just over a fortnight after Lincoln had taken his seat. They made no impression on Congress; no doubt Lincoln had not anticipated that they would. They represented his own view, and in addition they were part of his work for his party. But as the war with Mexico had been dragging on for twenty months, no one was interested now in how it had started. The resolutions did Lincoln harm in his own state, where the war had been supported energetically. His inquiries about the "spot" were ridiculed and were used against him. "Out damned spot," cried the Demoratic *Register* in Springfield, an opposition newspaper.

But he followed the resolutions up in the next month with a speech—his first important speech in the House—in which again he criticised the policy of the President. He analysed the whole question of the boundary dispute lucidly and he passed on to criticise the conduct of the war. It is quite a good speech to read. In addition he voted in favour of a resolution declaring that the Mexican War was "unnecessarily and unconstitutionally begun by the President of the United States." But this also did Lincoln harm at home, and made it certain that if he had tried to stand again for Congress he would not have been acceptable to his party organisation in Illinois. Indeed the Whigs were in difficulties over the Mexican War. They had started by criticising the manner of its beginning, but they had been forced by its success to moderate their criticism. They were careful to vote supplies to ensure its successful prosecution, and they devoted their criticisms to its conduct rather than to its moral justification.

The great issue which arose from the Mexican War was the question whether slavery should be extended to the newly acquired Territories. It did not come to its crisis while Lincoln was a member of Congress, but signs of its approach were already apparent and with them some idea of the attitude which Lincoln would take. The occasion for an expression of his view arose in relation to what was called the Wilmot Proviso. In August 1846, when the Mexican War had just begun, President Polk had asked the Twenty-Ninth Congress to appropriate two million dollars for the purchase of some more land from Mexico.[2] A disgruntled Northern Democrat in the House of Representatives, David Wilmot of Pennsylvania, introduced an amendment to the appropriation bill providing that "neither slavery nor involuntary servitude shall ever exist" in the Territory so acquired—copying the words of the North-West Ordinance of 1787. The Whigs and some other Northern Democrats joined forces and carried this amendment in the House, but the Senate rejected it.

In the succeeding Thirtieth Congress, that of which Lincoln was a member, the Wilmot Proviso was brought up repeatedly and the Whigs attempted to insert it into legislation whenever possible. Lincoln often said that he voted for the Wilmot Proviso in various forms forty or fifty times during his single term as Congressman. This was an exaggeration, and no doubt meant to be so, but it shows Lincoln's attitude to the spread of slavery. However, the Proviso was not carried and the problem of the extension of slavery into the newly acquired Territories remained to be solved.

Voting repeatedly for the Wilmot Proviso was not the only way in which Lincoln showed his attitude to the slavery question. In the second session of the Thirtieth Congress, which began in December 1848, Lincoln voted on various resolutions connected with the abolition of slavery or the slave trade in the District of Columbia. This District, in which the capital, Washington, was situated, had been formed by cessions from the states of Maryland and Virginia, and at the time when these cessions were made slavery existed in the ceded areas. But as it was now governed by Congress, slavery there could not be defended on the grounds of state sovereignty. There had been agitation for the abolition of slavery in the District, but Southern Congressmen and Senators naturally opposed it, and slave-dealers found it a useful place for carrying on their trade. In the Thirtieth Congress the movement for abolition grew strong, and in the second session resolutions were moved calling for bills to abolish either slavery in the District or the slave trade there. Lincoln actually voted *against* these resolutions. The only one he sup-

[2] It was proposed to make some payment to Mexico for any land ceded as a result of the war.

ported was a resolution which would have authorised a referendum of the people of the District on the question. He had definite ideas of his own on these questions, and he did not believe that unqualified abolition was wise.

At this stage Lincoln brought forward his own proposal, which he hoped might prove acceptable to both contending parties. He offered it as an amendment to a resolution against which he had voted, but which had been carried, calling for a bill to abolish slavery in the District. It had no effect upon the debate and it finds no place therefore in the history of the movement for abolishing slavery in the District of Columbia. But it deserves discussion in a life of Lincoln because the plan which he produced was a compromise. It was the proposal of a moderate man. It had also much in common with the resolutions he had moved in his protest in the Illinois legislature in 1837 and with the plans he put forward later on in the years of his Presidency. It gives us an interesting indication of the cautious and steady development of Lincoln's ideas upon slavery.

The essence of the compromise was, that while slavery was to be abolished in the District of Columbia, the process was to be gradual and the slave-owner to receive compensation for his loss. This was a principle he advocated later as President. At the same time he provided that the law should not come into force unless adopted by a popular vote in the District. Here was an echo of the protest of 1837. But the proposal was not accepted, although Lincoln claimed that it was supported by influential residents in the District. It was too moderate; neither side was in any mood for compromise.

This is about the total of Abraham Lincoln's achievement as a Congressman. Ambition and moderation had not produced much. He had done his usual routine duties, attending to the requests of his constituents, looking after the interests of his state, making recommendations for patronage when it came his way. In all this he appears to have acted honestly and satisfactorily. But his time in Congress had done almost nothing to advance his political career. His one short term was over. The leading Whig politicians in Illinois had agreed, before Lincoln's election, that each would sit for one term only and make way for the other at the end of the term.

No doubt Lincoln would have liked to be re-elected, but he was pledged to withdraw, and in any case, had he stood again, it is almost certain he would have been defeated. Lincoln himself had become unpopular by his attitude to the Mexican War, but the Whigs were also on the decline in Illinois. His former partner, Judge Logan, obtained the Whig nomination, but he was defeated in the election and the Democrats captured the seat.

The Whigs in the country at large, however, obtained some success. In the Presidential election of 1848 they elected General Zachary Taylor to the Presidency. Lincoln had done his part in supporting the Whig candidate, touring the states of New England to speak on his behalf, and concluding the campaign in his own district in Illinois. The tour in New England brought new experiences and contact with people whose way of life and whose views were new to him. But, with the success of the Whig candidate and his inauguration on March 4, 1849, Lincoln's period of office was over. He attempted to obtain the appointment of Commissioner of the General Land Office at Washington under the new administration, but he failed. A little later he was offered the governorship of the newly organised Territory of Oregon, but he declined it. He went back to Springfield and the law.

Lincoln was forty when he took up again the old life in Springfield. He spent most of his time away from his home. He was either on circuit with the judge or he was at his office, where he enjoyed the freedom to do as he pleased which was not available at home. He was not methodical or tidy in his business. He kept many of his documents in his tall silk hat; his office was not clean; there was no system of bookkeeping. On circuit the life was still hard. Until 1854 there was no railway in the country through which he had to travel; so he used a horse and buggy—the horse, it is said, "an indifferent, raw-boned specimen." One of Lincoln's biographers, Henry Bryan Binns, describes how "twice a year, in spring and early autumn, the judge accompanied by his band of lawyers would set forth from Springfield to visit the fifteen [fourteen] county seats of the circuit." The inns at which they stayed were the best that could be found, but they were not very comfortable. "The dignitaries of the court slept two in a hard bed, and sometimes eight in a room, several occupying the floor. Their ill-cooked meals were shared by labourers and pedlars, and even, on occasion, by the prisoner himself." Lincoln was more at home here than in his house at Springfield. He liked the talk and the company and the unhurried freedom. At the office his children came to see him and were permitted to behave as badly as they pleased. It is recorded that he liked his own children, but did not care for other people's. He had four boys—Robert Todd, born in 1843; Edward Baker, born in 1846; William Wallace, born in 1850; and Thomas ("Tad") born in 1853.[3] His partner Herndon says that "they were absolutely unrestrained in their amusement. . . . If they pulled down all the books from the shelves, bent the points of all the pens, overturned the spittoon, it never disturbed the serenity of their father's good nature." Herndon himself could not feel so benevolent.

So for some years he lived at Springfield, mixing with his own people on the frontier, discussing and listening and forming his mind slowly. He was a good lawyer—his prowess has usually been underrated or overstated—and he made a comfortable income from the law. And the law enriched and trained his mind. "His mind was like his body," said Herndon, "and worked slowly but strongly. Hence there was very little bodily or mental wear and tear in him. . . ." This analysis seems more and more accurate as his political career unfolds. For the present a picture of Lincoln as he was in the years after his retirement from Congress in 1849 is given well in the words of Herndon:

"He was not a pretty man by any means, nor was he an ugly one; he was a homely man, careless of his looks, plain-looking and plain acting. He had no aristocratic pomp, display or dignity, so called. He appeared simple in his carriage and bearing. He was a sad-looking man, his melancholy dripped from him as he walked. His apparent gloom impressed his friends, and created sympathy for him. He was

---

[3] Robert alone lived to manhood; he died in 1926 without surviving male issue; Edward died in 1850, William in 1862, while Lincoln was President, and "Tad" in 1871.

gloomy, abstracted and joyous—rather humorous—by turns, but I do not think he knew what real joy was for many years."

While this man of moderation and compromise lived far removed from national politics, practising the law, chopping his wood, milking his cow and caring for his raw-boned horse, telling his droll stories with almost relentless persistence, a great attempt at compromise was being undertaken at Washington. The problem of the Territories newly acquired from Mexico had still to be solved. The Wilmot Proviso, prohibiting slavery in any of these Territories, had been rejected by the Senate in the Twenty-Ninth Congress and it had not been passed in the Thirtieth Congress of which Lincoln was a member. But with the close of the war with Mexico and the Treaty of Guadalupe Hidalgo in 1848, the problem became acute. California, forming about a third of the country conquered from Mexico, applied in 1849 to be admitted to the Union as a free state. Gold had been discovered there in January 1848, just before the treaty of peace with Mexico had been signed, and thousands of immigrants poured in. It had organised itself into a state, had adopted a constitution, and the people had chosen a governor and legislature, which began to work in 1850.

But the proposal to admit California as a free state aroused such strong opposition from the South that for a time it looked as if the Union might be broken in two. It was indeed another of those times when the United States was half slave and half free. There were in 1849 fifteen free states and fifteen slave states. In the Senate, therefore, the South was evenly balanced with the North. In the House of Representatives, however, it was outnumbered and it seemed permanently so. The North had a population of almost fourteen million and it was increasing; the South had nine million—and nearly four million of these were slaves—and it stood fairly stationary. Any increase in the number of free states was therefore watched by the South with anxiety. Not that the South would oppose any increase in the number of free states. On the contrary it expected such an increase. But it was determined that no such increase should prevent permanently some possibility of increase in the number of slave states also.

The proposal to admit California as a free state did endanger the chance of Southern expansion. It meant that slavery was prohibited in about a third of the newly acquired country. Nor could the proposal be defended by regarding it as a mere extension still further of the line of the Missouri Compromise. By the Missouri Compromise it was agreed that there should be no slavery to the north of the line 36° 30′ latitude. But only half of California lay above this line; the rest lay below it. Here, said the South, is an invasion of the North into lands which we had a right to expect would be open to us under the Missouri Compromise. It is aggression and it is faithlessness. On the Northern side the principle of the Wilmot Proviso had captured political opinion. President Polk, before his term of office expired in March 1849, had recommended that the line of the Missouri Compromise should be extended to the new Territories, but his proposal was rejected. The extremists—represented particularly by the Abolitionists on one side, and the secessionists on the other—made this compromise inacceptable. Yet it would have been a proposal which the North could have accepted. For it was clear that little of the land gained from Mexico would be suitable for slave labour and the fears of the North were unfounded.

There was a gigantic battle in Congress—both in the House of Representatives and the Senate—over the question. It issued in the great compromise of 1850, sponsored by Henry Clay, the Whig leader. To the North there was made the concession of admitting California as a free state. This meant a modification of the principle of the Missouri Compromise, for slavery was now to be prohibited in an area below the line 36° 30′. It meant also sixteen free states to fifteen slave states. A second concession made to the North was the abolition of the slave trade—but not slavery itself—in the District of Columbia.

To the South two important concessions were made. Two new Territories—New Mexico and Utah—were to be organised with no stipulation as to whether they were to be slave or free, and the South was thus left to develop these Territories, if it could, into slave states. There was a chance and a hope, at any rate, that the balance might be restored in favour of the South. Here again there was a denial of the principle of the Missouri Compromise. The whole of the Territory of Utah lay to the north of the line 36° 30′, and even some part of the Territory of New Mexico also; if the terms of the Missouri Compromise had been extended to the new Territories, slavery would have been prohibited in Utah and in the north parts of New Mexico. California had been a modification of the Missouri Compromise in favour of the North; here was a modification of the Missouri Compromise in favour of the South.

The second concession made to the South was the enactment of a new and stricter Fugitive Slave Law. The Southern states complained that the North had failed in its duty to facilitate the return to their owners of slaves who had escaped. They demanded a guarantee that their property would be safeguarded. The new law made it possible for escaped slaves to be recaptured anywhere in the United States, brought before Federal courts and, if proof of ownership was established, to be returned to their owners by officers of the United States—the Federal Marshals—who could call upon citizens to assist them in the execution of their duty if necessary. A slave brought before a court in this way was not allowed to testify on his own behalf. The North disliked this law. It was part of the compromise which they found it hardest to accept. Had it not been for the support which Daniel Webster, the venerable Whig lawyer, gave to Clay in the Senate, the North would not have accepted it. Webster's support of the compromise was denounced in savage and angered terms by the uncompromising section. It moved J. G. Whittier, the American poet, to write "Ichabod," lamenting the shame and dishonour of Webster's action:

> "All else is gone; from these great eyes
>   The soul has fled:
> When faith is lost, when honor dies,
>   The man is dead."

To Whittier and those who shared his outlook there could be no more compromise about slavery.

Many in the North and South who disliked the Compromise of 1850 held this view. They were prepared to say, as Lincoln said eight years later: "This Union cannot endure half slave and half free"; and they were prepared to add what Lincoln would not add: "Let the Union cease. Let the slave states go their way, and let the free states go theirs." There were those in the North who, because they hated slavery, were prepared to see the Union cease, if by so doing they could prevent the extension of slavery. And there were those in the South who defended slavery so fiercely that they were prepared to see the Union cease, if by so doing they could preserve slavery and if possible extend it.

To these extreme people, in North and South, the Compromise of 1850 was a betrayal or a dishonour or an injury. But Clay and Webster had finally carried the Compromise. It looked as if once more the crical issue which might have divided the Union had been averted by compromise. For a time there was tranquillity in Washington, just as in Springfield there was tranquillity for Lincoln. There was peace for the nation. As Professor S. E. Morison has put it in his *History of the United States*: "Once more the Union was preserved by the same spirit of compromise that created it; but for the last time."

Chapter 4

"An Irrepressible Conflict"

"Oh Kansas, bleeding Kansas,
You will not let me rest!"
STEPHEN VINCENT BENÉT: *John Brown's Body.*

THE COMPROMISE OF 1850 seemed likely to mark the beginning of a new chapter in the history of the making of the American Union. As if to symbolise the departure of old antagonisms, there had occurred in March 1850, before the final compromise had been achieved, the death of John C. Calhoun, the unrelenting and passionate Southern leader, who had threatened the secession of the South if it was not satisfied upon the slavery issue. For a while the slavery issue sank into the background. But it became evident that the Compromise had not marked the beginning of a new chapter; it had really marked the end of an old one. For if a strong threat to the Union had departed in the person of Calhoun, strong supports of the Union also disappeared. On June 29, 1852, Henry Clay died, and on October 24 of the same year Daniel Webster died. The two great symbols of compromise were gone. And it was already apparent that the struggle was about to begin again. It was "an irrepressible conflict."[1]

In the years from 1850 to 1858 the American Union moved steadily forward to a crisis in its affairs. As the crisis drew nearer, Abraham Lincoln came to be roused from his peaceful and ruminating seclusion to think and speak upon the great political issues of his time. In this chapter he will be seen to emerge again into national politics as one event after another pushed the Union forward to its crisis. There were, indeed, four great events that contributed to this crisis, and each must be treated in turn.

[1] The words of William H. Seward in a speech on October 25, 1858, to which reference will be made later. See pp. 66–67.

The first event which led to a crisis was the writing of a book. In June 1851 *Uncle Tom's Cabin*, by Harriet Beecher Stowe, began as a serial in *The National Era*, an abolitionist newspaper in Washington. It ran throughout that year and continued into the spring of 1852. On March 20 it was published as a book, and it was a sensational success; 300,000 copies were sold in the first year. *Uncle Tom's Cabin* was the most influential piece of printed matter which appeared in the United States directed against the institution of slavery, and consequently against the states of the South which supported that institution. No other document in the whole scheme of propaganda was so effective. It was one of the four great factors which made compromise upon the slavery question out of date.

Ten years later Mrs. Stowe was to go to the White House and to be received by President Abraham Lincoln with the words: "So you're the little woman who wrote the book that made this great war." She and he were then probably the two best-known Americans throughout the world, as Carl Sandburg, Lincoln's great modern biographer, has said. She became a strong and faithful friend to Lincoln and a supporter of his policy. But this was in the future. In 1852 *Uncle Tom's Cabin* had burst upon America. We do not know when Lincoln read it; we can assume, surely, that he did. It is worth while for a student of the life of Abraham Lincoln to read it once more in these days. He will be surprised, perhaps, to see how fairly the picture is drawn. Uncle Tom has many masters, but only one is bad and cruel; the attitude of the Northern states to negroes is frankly presented—they disapprove of slavery, but they do not love negroes; nor are all slaves presented as good and honest. But, of course, it was the brutality of Simon Legree, the overseer, and the tragedy of the selling of slaves and the break-up of families, which stood out most vividly to the Northern reader. What was exceptional in the system, in the eyes of the South, came to be accepted as the general rule in the eyes of the North. And the very moderation of the book, when its moderation was recognised, strengthened the influence which it exercised.

The second great factor in bringing on the crisis was the passing of an act of Congress—the Kansas-Nebraska Act of

1854. This act arose from beginnings which looked innocent enough, although they involved a conflict of interest between North and South. The question at issue was the route of a transcontinental railway. Among the many schemes that had been proposed, there were four of particular importance, and Congress in March 1853 authorised surveys of these four routes under the direction of the War Department. The first was the northern route, from the Upper Mississippi to the Upper Missouri, and thence across to the Columbia river; the second was the central route, from St. Louis up the Kansas and Arkansas rivers, across the Rocky Mountains to the Great Salt Lake and thence to San Francisco; the third was known as the thirty-fifth parallel route, and ran from Memphis, up the Arkansas and Canadian rivers, across the Rocky Mountains near Santa Fé and through the Apache and Mojave country to Los Angeles; and the fourth was the southern route, from New Orleans up the Red river and across Texas, and by the Grilla valley to Yuma and San Diego.[2]

The first two of these routes would be of advantage to the North, and in particular, so far as the slavery question was concerned, they would link with the North the free state of California and future free state of Oregon. The great obstacle to the construction of a railway on either of these two routes was that a large tract of Indian country lay between, which so far had not been organised under Territorial Governments. The southern route had many advantages, and appealed especially to the Southern States. It was the shortest route to the coast; it lay through states and Territories which were already organised, and the country to be traversed was more suitable for railway construction than the country in the North. It made available to the South an opportunity for development which might compensate it in some measure for what it had lost in the Compromise of 1850.

[2] The line of these routes cannot easily be followed without a map, and, although the details are not important in the understanding of the Kansas-Nebraska Act, it may be well to say that a good map of the routes can be found in S. E. Morison's *History of the United States* or in S. E. Morison and H. S. Commager's *The Growth of the American Republic*.

The first move towards getting Congress to adopt the southern route was taken on the initiative of Jefferson Davis, Secretary of War under the administration of President Franklin Pierce, a Democrat, who had taken office in 1853. Jefferson Davis later became President of the states which seceded from the Union, and it is interesting to find him at this stage involved in an event which later influenced his own career. He saw that the railway on the southern route would have to pass through some part of Mexican territory, and he therefore induced President Pierce to buy the territory involved for ten million dollars. The purchase, known as the Gadsden Purchase, was completed by a treaty in December 1853, the last step in the extension of the boundaries of the continental United States to what they are at this day. With this purchase everything seemed ready for the adoption by Congress of the southern route.

At this stage Stephen A. Douglas, the senior Senator for Illinois and Lincoln's old associate and rival in the back room of Joshua Speed's store in Springfield, brought forward a plan to ensure the adoption of the central route, the second of the routes outlined above. Douglas himself had speculated in the lands through which the central route would pass, and he stood to gain personally through its adoption. But he supported the proposal also as a representative of Illinois, which the line might be expected to benefit. The difficulty which supporters of the central route had to face was the existence of a stretch of country through which the line must pass which had not been organised under any sort of government. Douglas brought forward a bill in January 1854 to organise the great plains of the Louisiana Purchase, lying to the west of the states of Iowa and Missouri, as the Territory of Nebraska, with a territorial legislature. But this by itself would not receive the support of the South. The whole of the proposed Territory lay above the line 36° 30′, and by the terms of the Missouri Compromise it must remain free. The Territory of Nebraska when it came to be created would be one more free government. To meet this opposition Douglas proposed in his bill that the principle of what he called "popular sovereignty" should apply. It was to rest with the people of the new Territory to decide whether or not they would have slavery. This was, after all, what had been done in the Compromise of 1850 in regard to New Mexico and Utah. It was a contradiction of the principle of the Missouri Compromise, of course, but that had been done in 1850 also, and in any case it was argued that, in fact, slavery would never be introduced into Nebraska because the climate and the soil were not suitable for cotton cultivation. The Territory would, in fact, be free, but the South would feel that they had a possibility of extending slavery there.

Some amendments were necessary before Douglas could get sufficient support from the South. He divided the proposed new Territory into two parts—Nebraska, to the west of Iowa, which was a free state and was likely therefore to send immigrants into Nebraska and make it a free Territory, and Kansas, west of Missouri, which would be expected to make it a slave Territory. Then it was found that the Senators from the slave states of Kentucky and Missouri were not satisfied with the mere implied repeal of the Missouri Compromise which Douglas's bill would effect. They wished for an explicit repeal of the act which established the Missouri Compromise. Douglas accepted this proposal. Davis gladly gave up his advocacy of the southern route in return for this removal of the ban on slavery and the repeal of the Missouri Compromise. The Kansas-Nebraska Act passed through Congress and received the assent of President Pierce on May 30, 1854.

Douglas's proposals had been received with bitter and violent hostility in the North. The debate in Congress dragged on for three months, and when the bill was at last passed, North and South had deepened their enmity of each other. It was the repeal of the Missouri Compromise that was hated and feared most in the North, the going back upon an agreement of thirty years' standing that slavery should not be extended north of the line 36° 30'. If that was the price of saving the Union, there were those in the North who felt that it was not worth saving.

The Kansas-Nebraska Act brought Lincoln back to politics and made him known for the first time outside his own state. "In 1854," he recorded of himself, "his profession had almost superseded the thought of politics in his mind, when the repeal of the Missouri Compromise aroused him as he had never been before." His chance came when Douglas visited the state of Illinois in October 1854 and spoke in defence of his bill and of the principle of popular sovereignty or "squatter" sovereignty, as it came to be called. On October 3 Douglas spoke at Springfield, and the next day Lincoln answered him in a speech of three hours. On October 16 Douglas spoke at the town of Peoria, and that evening Lincoln answered him, delivering the speech which he had given at Springfield twelve days before, but with some corrections and additions. This speech at Peoria is the first of his great speeches, and it first made him known outside his own state.

Lincoln's argument in this speech reveals once more that mixture of the uncompromising attitude on the moral issue and the attitude of compromise on the political issue which had characterised his earlier and less mature attempts at dealing with the question. He asserts boldly that slavery is wrong and that therefore nobody ought to adopt an attitude of indifference to it. He says, further, that slavery must not be exended into the Territories:

"The law which forbids the bringing of slaves *from* Africa, and that which has so long forbid the taking them *to* Nebraska, can hardly be distinguished on any moral principle, and the repeal of the former could find quite as plausible excuses as that of the latter. . . ."

That is one side of the question. But on the other side he is still no Abolitionist. He sees the difficulty of getting rid of slavery where it exists.

"When Southern people tell us they are no more responsible for the origin of slavery than we, I acknowledge the fact. When it is said that the institution exists, and that it is very difficult to get rid of it in any satisfactory way, I can understand and appreciate the saying. I surely will not blame them for not doing what I should not know how to do myself. If all earthly power were given me, I should not know what to do as to the existing institution. . . . It does seem to me that systems of gradual emancipation might be adopted; but for their tardiness in this I will not undertake to judge our brethren of the South. When they remind us of their constitutional rights, I acknowledge them, not grudgingly, but fully and fairly; and I would give them any legislation for the reclaiming of their fugitives which should not, in its stringency, be more likely to carry a free man into slavery, than our ordinary criminal laws are to hang an innocent one."

Lincoln was prepared to put up with the existence of slavery in the South and to grant a stringent Fugitive Slave Law, but he would not tolerate the extension of slavery into the Territories. But against his position one argument was directed to which he had to find an answer. Suppose, he was asked, that the South refuses to remain in the Union if it is not allowed some possibility of extending slavery into the Territories, what would you say then? Is not the Kansas-Nebraska Act a great measure for saving the Union by satisfying the South? Do you prefer to keep slavery out of the Territories and break the Union, rather than to admit slavery and save the Union? Which do you choose, the extension of slavery or the breaking of the Union? To this Lincoln answered that if these were really the alternatives which the Kansas-Nebraska Act held out, he would choose the extension of slavery and the maintenance of the Union. "Much as I hate slavery, I would consent to the extension of it rather than see the Union dissolved, just as I would consent to any great evil to avoid a greater one."

This was a startling answer. It is a sentence to remember. It guides Lincoln's thought. It is the saving of the American Union which is always uppermost in his thoughts and policy. But in this case he goes on quickly to complete the answer. He says he does not believe that these are the alternatives which are presented. It is not true to claim that the extension of slavery, by such measures as the Kansas-Nebraska Act, will save the Union. Such measures may persuade the South that it is worth while to remain in the Union, but will they not also go far to persuade the North that it is becoming fast a Union in which it is not worth while to remain? "When I go to Union-saving," says Lincoln, "I must believe, at least, that the means I employ have some adaptation to the end. To my mind Nebraska has no such adaptation. . . . It is an aggravation, rather, of the only one thing which ever endangers the Union."

Lincoln here had touched upon the heart of the problem —whether the Union could survive half slave and half free. Some in the South had come to claim that the extension of slavery was necessary if they were to remain in the Union; some in the North asserted that if slavery was extended, they would leave the Union. These extreme positions were coming to be occupied. Lincoln wrote to a friend at this time: "Our political problem now is, Can we, as a nation, continue together permanently—for ever—half slave and half free? The problem is too mighty for me. May God, in His mercy, superintend the solution." Here was his first expression of the startling declaration that was to come about three years later.

The Kansas-Nebraska Act had roused Lincoln. He became in his state the leader of the Whigs in their attack upon Douglas and his doctrines. In 1855 Douglas's colleague from Illinois in the United States Senate, James Shields, reached the end of his term of office. Lincoln came forward as a Whig candidate, but when he saw that he could not obtain a majority, he advised his Whig followers to support Lyman Trumbull, an anti-Nebraska Democrat. Trumbull was elected and took his place with Douglas, though opposed to him, as a Senator from Illinois. Lincoln was keenly disappointed at his defeat; indeed, after having been elected in 1854 to the Illinois state legislature, he had resigned soon after in order to be elected as Senator. Yet had he been chosen, his later contest with Douglas, of which we shall read in the next chapter, would not have occurred and Lincoln's fame might well have been less.

If popular sovereignty was to settle whether Kansas should be slave or free, it became important that the Territory should be occupied as soon as possible by people who could be relied upon to vote it slave or free. So there began at once a contest to capture the Territory. Pro-slavery emigrants began to cross into Kansas from Missouri; thereupon there was organised a movement of emigration of Northerners. There were clashes between the rival contingents. In May 1856, at Potawatomie in Kansas, an old man named John Brown, with some of his sons, attacked the homes of pro-slavery families in the Territory and murdered five men. It was a savage, fanatical crime. Pro-slavery men retaliated, and one of John Brown's sons was killed. This John Brown will be heard of again. The Missourians sacked the first settlement of the Northerners at Lawrence. There were reports of massacres. There was talk of "bleeding Kansas." Feeling between North and South was increasingly inflamed as the rival forces in Kansas prepared to exercise the right of popular sovereignty.

In May 1856 the Kansas quarrel led to an incident in the chamber of the United States Senate which ranks as the third great event which brought on the crisis. On May 19 Charles Sumner, a Senator from Massachusetts and a strong opponent of slavery and of slavery extension, made a speech on "The crime against Kansas." There was much in the speech that was true and some things that were not true. But the speech contained some disgraceful personal attacks upon Senator Butler, of South Carolina, who was absent. Three days later, on May 22, a young Southerner, Preston Brooks, a member of the House of Representatives and a kinsman of Senator Butler, walked into the Senate chamber and attacked Senator Sumner as he sat at his desk. He beat him over the head with a cane, inflicting serious injuries, and Sumner was left practically unconscious. The incident provoked the most violent feelings in North and South. The South welcomed Brooks as a hero. He was presented with inscribed canes by his admirers in South Carolina. In the North the resentment was deep. Sumner was, next to Seward, the foremost leader of the North. It has been declared by a biographer of Abraham Lincoln, Albert J. Beveridge, that the beating of Sumner by Brooks was as much a factor in bringing on the Civil War in the United States as was *Uncle Tom's Cabin* and Kansas. It made the North feel that union with the South on such terms was intolerable.

But the Sumner-Brooks incident combined with the continued Kansas agitation had an immediate result which was important for the career of Lincoln. It made possible the survival and growth of a new political party, organised to oppose the extension of slavery and destined to replace the

Whigs—the Republican party. It seems that the Republican party was born on July 6, 1854, at a convention held under the oaks at a place called Jackson in the state of Michigan. But many places claim its birth. At any rate, it was at Jackson that the name Republican was chosen, the name by which Jefferson's party had been known when first it was formed in opposition to the Federalists and before it split later and became the Democratic party. The new Republican party was brought into existence by the Kansas-Nebraska controversy; it was formed to combat the extension of slavery. But at first it did not gain much ground. The Whigs held aloof from it, for they were by no means united in their attitude to slavery; those Democrats who opposed their party on the Kansas-Nebraska issue were not yet prepared to join in any new party; and the existing anti-slavery parties did not wish to lose their identity in yet one more new anti-slavery organisation. Thus it was that when, in October 1854, the Abolitionists in Lincoln's home town of Springfield held a meeting, calling themselves by the name of Republicans, and invited Lincoln to attend it, he was careful to go out of town that day and avoid alliance with them. He was still a Whig.

Two years of Kansas agitation, culminating in the Sumner-Brooks affair, made a great difference. On May 29, 1856, Lincoln attended the State Convention of the Republican party at Bloomington, Illinois. For some time his mind had been moving towards a party organised to withstand the extension of slavery; that was becoming the predominant issue in his mind. Whether it was Lincoln's partner Herndon who finally forced his hand by putting Lincoln's name to a circular calling a meeting to appoint delegates to the State Convention is open to doubt. Herndon claimed that he supplied the push needed to bring Lincoln over. We may be certain that Lincoln knew where he was going, though he was slow to take the plunge. The party organisation in Illinois needed a leader to bind together its diverse elements—Whigs, anti-Nebraska Democrats, Abolitionists, and "Know-nothings," the last a secret, anti-Catholic and anti-foreigner organisation. Lincoln seized this opportunity for leadership in his speech to the Bloomington Convention—a speech of which there is no authentic record and which is usually referred to as "The Lost Speech." He was nominated as a Presidential elector on the Republican ticket, and from now on was formally and openly an adherent of the Republican party.

In the next month the first National Convention of the Republican party to nominate a candidate for the Presidential election was held at Philadelphia. The Convention nominated a popular explorer, John C. Frémont, as Presidential candidate and William L. Dayton as Vice-Presidential candidate. In the contest for nomination as Vice-Presidential candidate, Lincoln proved to be Dayton's most serious rival, for he received 110 votes in the Convention. It was fortunate that he did not succeed, for the future of a Vice-Presidential candidate in the United States, whether he succeeds or fails in the election, has usually been obscure, if we except the rare cases where the Vice-President has succeeded to the Presidency on the death of the President. As it was, Lincoln appears to have been surprised that he obtained so many votes. When told of it he said, "It must be the other great man of the same name from Massachusetts."

Frémont, who was defeated by James Buchanan, the Democratic candidate, is noteworthy as the first Republican Presidential candidate; Abraham Lincoln was the second. James Buchanan is noteworthy as the last Democratic President of the United States for nearly thirty years. So had the Republican party grown, and so near was it to victory in the national government. Indeed, in November 1856 Buchanan polled only 400,000 votes more than Frémont, while the combined votes of Frémont and Fillmore, the candidate of the Whigs and the Know-nothings, was 400,000 in excess of Buchanan's. If the opponents of the Democrats could unite, victory was possible. In December 1856 the Republican party, feeling that, though it had lost the Presidential election, it had gained in strength, held a banquet at Chicago, and Lincoln was one of those who spoke.

Within a day or two of President Buchanan's inauguration, on March 4, 1857, the fourth and final great event which deserves attention occurred. This was the judgment of the Supreme Court of the United States in the Dred Scott case. In this case, known technically as *Dred Scott v. Sandford*,[3] a negro, Dred Scott, asked the Supreme Court to declare that he was a free man. Scott was a slave; his master had taken him from Missouri, a slave state, to Illinois, a free state, and thence into the Territory of Wisconsin, north of the line 36° 30′, where, by the Missouri Compromise, slavery was not to be permitted. Thereafter Scott was taken back to Missouri, and he sued for his freedom on the ground that he had resided on free soil. The case came finally to the Supreme Court. It was full of technicalities, and it seems clear that it could have been decided against Scott on one of these technicalities. Instead, however, the Court chose to decide the wider issues of slavery. It held, by a majority, that Scott's claim to freedom must fail on three grounds; first, as a negro he could not be a citizen of the United States, and therefore he had no right to sue in a Federal court; secondly, as a resident of Missouri he was not affected in any way by the laws of Illinois, and therefore could claim no freedom from the free laws of Illinois; and thirdly, his residence in territory above the line 36° 30′ did not make him free, because Congress had no power to prohibit slavery in the national Territories. From this third point it followed that the Missouri Compromise was unconstitutional. The great assumption that Congress could prevent the extension of slavery to the Territories was declared to be without foundation. Kansas, Nebraska, Oregon were all open to slavery; Congress could not prevent it. All that were needed were sufficient pro-slavery squatters, invading from the South, and a vote for slavery could be carried in any Territory.

[3] A misspelling in the official report for Sanford.

Chapter 5

The Lincoln-Douglas Debates

"No—he ain't much on looks—or much on speed—
A young dog can outrun him any time,
Outlook him and outeat him and outleap him,
But, Mister, that dog's hell on a cold scent
And, once he gets his teeth in what he's after,
He don't let go until he knows he's dead."
STEPHEN VINCENT BENÉT: *John Brown's Body*.

WHAT WAS THE good of the doctrine of popular sovereignty now? The Dred Scott decision had laid it down that Congress could not prohibit slavery in the Territories of the United States. It must follow from this, surely, that no Territorial legislature set up by Congress could prohibit slavery within the confines of its Territory. It had no choice; it must permit slavery. This robbed Douglas's doctrine of any value it may ever have had of attracting the support of those who, while not Abolitionists, opposed the further extension of slavery. But Douglas was not disposed to take this reverse lying down. He proceeded at once to try to minimise the effects of the decision.

His first attempt was foreshadowed in a speech he made on June 12, 1857, in Springfield, a few months after the Supreme Court's decision. He defended the decision, and then went on to try to reconcile the decision with the working of popular sovereignty. He discussed the basis of a master's right to his slave in the Territory of Kansas, and then said:

"While the right continues in full force under the guarantees of the Constitution, and cannot be diverted or alienated by an act of Congress, it necessarily remains a barren and worthless right unless sustained, protected and enforced by appropriate police regulations and local legislation prescribing adequate remedies for its violation. These regulations and remedies must necessarily depend entirely upon the will and wishes of the people of the Territory, as they can only be prescribed by the local legislatures. Hence, the great principle of popular sovereignty and self-government is sustained and firmly established by the authority of this decision."

This was the first statement of a doctrine, to become famous in the next year as the "Freeport Doctrine." It suggested that a Territory might be able to evade the consequences of the Dred Scott decision by refraining from passing the laws to enforce the institution of slavery. On this point Abraham Lincoln was to concentrate in his contest with Douglas in the coming years. For the present it needs to be noted as an attempt by Douglas to make the best of popular sovereignty after the set-back of the Dred Scott decision.

But there was one other way in which popular sovereignty could be defended. Although, by the Dred Scott decision, Congress or a Territorial legislature could not prohibit slavery in a Territory, state constitutions could permit or prohibit slavery. The Dred Scott decision had no effect upon them. So while popular sovereignty might not seem to have much scope among the people of a Territory while it was a Territory, it would become operative when they were preparing a constitution with a view to being admitted as a state of the Union. Not that this arrangement gave much comfort to those who opposed the extension of slavery. It meant that the people of a Territory in which the institution of slavery was legal, and in which it might already exist, were to be expected to decide, when they prepared their constitution for admission as a state, that the institution of slavery should no longer exist within its borders. In some cases this might be effected fairly easily; in some Territories slavery, though permissible, would not have taken root. But it would not be easy in all.

Meanwhile Douglas had an opportunity of asserting his doctrine of popular sovereignty in the case of Kansas. The people of the Territory and the legislature of the Territory could not prevent slavery there, by the Dred Scott decision, but they could decide whether or not they should ask to be admitted into the Union as a slave state or a free state. There was controversy in the Territory for some years on this question. The details are confused and complicated. The essential points are that each side, the free-state party and the pro-slavery party, had drawn up a constitution, and had sent it to Congress asking to be admitted to the Union as a state. The free-state constitution was drawn up at a place called Topeka, in the Territory, and the slave-state constitution was drawn up at Lecompton. The Topeka Constitution was considered by Congress in 1856, under the administration of President Pierce, before President Buchanan's election. The House of Representatives was prepared to approve the Constitution, but the Senate rejected it. In 1857 the Lecompton Constitution came before Congress. Here Douglas came forward to assert the doctrine of popular sovereignty. He said that the Lecompton Constitution must be submitted to a fair and free vote of the people of the Territory. Congress should have nothing to do with any partisan production.

"Ignore Lecompton," he said, "ignore Topeka, treat both these party movements as irregular and void; pass a fair bill—the one that we framed ourselves when we were acting as a unit; have a fair election—and you will have peace in the Democratic party." Douglas prevailed after a long struggle, and the Lecompton Constitution was submitted to a vote of the people in Kansas. On January 4, 1858, they rejected it decisively.

Here, indeed, is an example of the passions that were being aroused on the slavery issue. Kansas and Nebraska both had a majority of anti-slavery people; in the end, they would make Kansas and Nebraska free states, although as Territories they were unable to prohibit slavery. But in the meanwhile every device that could be adopted to extend slavery was being adopted and the feelings between North and South were being made increasingly hostile. What the North feared was that gradually, throughout the Union, slavery would become legal, though the institution itself might not flourish everywhere; what the South feared was that gradually slavery might be made illegal everywhere.

And it was this issue which marked the crisis, and which Abraham Lincoln now took up. His opportunity came in 1858, when the time had come round for Douglas to seek re-election to the Senate as one of the Senators from Illinois.

His resistance to his own party and to President Buchanan over the Lecompton Constitution and his insistence on the submission of the issue to popular sovereignty had caused a break between him and the Democratic leaders. The election in Illinois was therefore of great significance. It was a test of Douglas's position. If he succeeded, he would be able to stand up against the Southern wing of his party and moderate their demands for the extension of slavery. It was a great opportunity for Lincoln also. On June 16, 1858, he was chosen by the Illinois Republican Convention, meeting at Springfield, as their candidate for the Senate against Douglas.

That evening Lincoln made a speech which was of great importance. He stated in memorable words the crisis which had been reached upon the issue of slavery. In his view the long-drawn-out controversy since 1854 upon the application of the Kansas-Nebraska Act had shown that the United States was divided between those who were resolved upon extending slavery throughout the whole country and those who were resolved that it should one day exist no more. One concise passage is worth quotation:

"We are now far into the fifth year, since a policy was initiated, with the avowed object, and confident promise, of putting an end to slavery agitation. Under the operation of that policy, that agitation has not only not ceased, but has constantly augmented. In my opinion it will not cease until a crisis shall have been reached and passed. 'A house divided against itself cannot stand.' I believe this government cannot endure, permanently half slave and half free. I do not expect the Union to be dissolved—I do not expect the house to fall—but I do expect it will cease to be divided. It will become all one thing, or all the other. Either the opponents of slavery will arrest the further spread of it, and place it where the public mind shall rest in the belief that it is in course of ultimate extinction, or its advocates will push it forward till it shall become alike lawful in all the states, old as well as new, North as well as South."

This was a provocative declaration. It ranks with the words which Seward was to use later in the same year, on October 25, 1858, when he said:

"Shall I tell you what this collision means? They who think

that it is . . . the work of . . . fanatical agitators, and therefore ephemeral, mistake the case altogether. It is an irrepressible conflict between opposing and enduring forces, and it means that the United States must . . . become either entirely a slave-holding nation or entirely a free-labor nation."

Phrases like this contributed to the very crisis which they prophesied; they exacerbated feeling and made compromise less likely than ever. In Seward's case they gave rise to the impression that he was an extremist and they assisted in defeating him for the Republican nomination as Presidential candidate in 1860, for he was the leading Republican and extremist utterances from him were more important and more damaging than from a relatively unknown man like Lincoln. But Lincoln found his "House-Divided" speech a cause of great trouble and embarrassment, and he was obliged to spend a lot of time explaining it.[1]

The fact is that it was not only an inexpedient and unwise utterance; it was of doubtful truth. After all, what chance was there of slavery extending to the Northern states? There was none at all. So far as certain Territories were concerned, it was possible, as in Kansas, for corrupt methods to be used in an attempt to secure the Territory's admission as a slave state and for these methods conceivably to succeed, but whether slavery would flourish in these states would depend upon economic and climatic factors. So that even as prophecy Lincoln's statement was almost certainly incorrect. Apart from this, its effect was inflammatory. It inflamed the North by its threat that sooner or later slavery would prevail, and the South by its threat (which seemed to them also a hope and an intention on Lincoln's side) that slavery would be abolished utterly. Then the quotation, "A house divided against itself cannot stand," seemed to envisage the break-up of the Union, but Lincoln hastened to rule out that possibility. In so doing, he denied to the extremists of North and South the consolations of secession; it was to be impossible for one side to say to the other: "Go in peace." The whole effect of

[1] About a month later, on July 10, 1858, at Chicago, for example, Lincoln said that by this declaration he did not intend it to be thought that he "was in favour of anything." It was "a prediction only—it may have been a foolish one perhaps."

the passage was to picture two irreconcilable forces indissolubly confined within the boundaries of the Union unable to compromise, unable to escape, with no prospect but unconditional surrender.

Lincoln's friends had advised him to delete this inflammatory passage from his speech, but he had steadfastly refused. Somehow the scriptural text had caught his imagination; he could not bring himself to sacrifice his carefully considered paragraph. No doubt the struggle against Douglas influenced him here. He must show that Douglas's popular sovereignty was dangerous, both for those who wished to prevent the extension of slavery, and those who wished to promote it. It could be used by either side to achieve its purposes. To the Republicans of the North Lincoln said: "Do not be tempted to follow Douglas and his apparently fair and democratic methods. By these methods slavery will be introduced in all the territories, as Kansas shows. Douglas may not want slavery in Kansas, but his popular sovereignty will allow it to be brought there." To the Democrats of the South Lincoln hoped to address some words which would undermine still further Douglas's position with them. He was to do this more effectively later in his attack on the "Freeport Doctrine," but for the present he confined himself to the assertion that the Union might become all free, and that no doctrine of popular sovereignty would avail to save slavery in the South.

It is not easy to explain all that Lincoln had in mind in steadfastly retaining this passage in his speech, but one strong reason appears to have been this hostility to Douglas and this determination at all costs to discredit his doctrine of popular sovereignty. Douglas was indeed a serious rival to Lincoln for the leadership of the Republican party in Illinois. There were many Republicans who would have accepted him, especially after he had broken with Buchanan and the Democrats over their handling of the Lecompton Constitution. But even if Douglas had refused to leave his party, he could have won over many votes to his side and thus dealt the young Republican party in Illinois a fatal blow. Lincoln saw this, and realised that his own future as well as that of his party in the state was at stake. Throughout his debates with Douglas he stresses their differences. To the student looking back now, the extent of their common ground is more striking than their differences. Douglas did not want to see slavery extended, nor did Lincoln; he did not propose to interfere with slavery in the states, nor did Lincoln; he did not like the decision of the Supreme Court in the Dred Scott case, nor did Lincoln. His Kansas-Nebraska Bill was an attempt at a compromise on the same principles as the Compromise of 1850; above all, he wished to save the Union, as Lincoln did. The pro-slavery secessionists of the South hated him even more than they hated Lincoln. These things should be remembered as we follow the debates.

Lincoln had begun his campaign for the Senatorship by the "House-Divided" speech at Springfield on June 16, 1858. On July 9 Douglas made a speech in Chicago. Lincoln was present: he took notes of what Douglas said, and the next day he made a speech in reply at the same place. Then Douglas spoke at an open-air meeting at Springfield on July 17, and Lincoln replied in the evening at a meeting in the State Hall of Representatives. But by this time Lincoln's supporters were becoming rather dissatisfied at the way in which Lincoln was following Douglas, always appearing in the wake of the great Democratic leader and never, so to speak, standing upon his own independent ground. They urged Lincoln to challenge Douglas to a series of debates. He agreed to the suggestion, and it was arranged that they should address the same meetings at seven towns in the state of Illinois on dates fixed throughout August, September and October. The procedure was that, alternately, one should speak an hour to open the debate, the other should have an hour and a half to reply, and the first should then have half an hour to finish. So the debates were held, at Ottawa on August 21, at Freeport on August 27, at Jonesboro on September 15, at Charleston on September 18, at Galesburg on October 7, at Quincy on October 13 and at Alton on October 15.[2]

---

[2] In addition to these formal debates both candidates addressed dozens of other meetings individually. It was at one of these meetings, at Clinton, on September 8, that Lincoln is alleged to have said: "You can fool all of the people some of the time and some of the people all the time, but you cannot fool all the people all

These Lincoln-Douglas debates aroused great interest in the state of Illinois and far outside it. The great issue before the American Union—whether it was to be a free Union or a slave Union—was debated by the two leaders. Yet it cannot be pretended that much pleasure can be obtained from reading the debates in full after the lapse of years. At times there are passages where the issues at stake stand out clearly and are stated with a force and clarity that cannot be surpassed. But much of the time is taken up, inevitably, with controversy on smaller points, with refutations and denials, with dissection of opponents' arguments and criticism of the opponents' parties. There are, in the nature of the case, many "debating" points to be scored. And indeed it is too much to expect that either contestant could sustain seven debates without much repetition. There is no need, therefore, for a detailed examination of the debates on each occasion. It is enough to concentrate upon the outstanding points. Three in particular are selected for discussion.

The people of Illinois were not unanimous in their attitude to the slavery question. In the north, where immigration from free states had largely determined the composition of the people, opinion was opposed to slavery; in the south, where immigration from slave states had occurred, there was correspondingly an opinion in its favour; while in the centre, where the Whigs were still strong, advocates of extreme abolitionism had caused many people to react in favour of the Democratic party. Lincoln and Douglas had to walk carefully among the varied opinions, and on the whole it looked as if Douglas could count on the greater support. For Lincoln it was most important to appear as a moderate if he was not to alienate central Illinois, but not too moderate if he was to retain the support of northern Illinois, where the Abolitionists might oppose him.

At the start of the debates Douglas made use of this dilemma. The first debate was at Ottawa, in northern Illinois, and there Douglas put these questions to Lincoln:

"1. Was he in favour of the repeal of the fugitive slave law?

the time." See, e.g. Carl Sandburg, *Lincoln, The Prairie Years*, vol. 2, p. 142.

"2. Was he pledged against the admission of any more slave states to the Union?

"3. Was he pledged against the admission of new states into the Union with such a constitution as the people of that state may see fit to make?

"4. Was he pledged to the abolition of slavery in the District of Columbia?

"5. Was he pledged to the prohibition of the slave trade between the different states?

"6. Was he pledged to prohibit slavery in all the Territories of the United States, north as well as south of the line of the Missouri Compromise?

"7. Was he opposed to the acquisition of any new Territory unless slavery is first prohibited therein?"

These were difficult questions for a man to answer who wished to be elected to a Senatorship by a state like Illinois. Northern Illinois might have liked him to say "Yes" to them all; southern Illinois might have required the answer "No" in all cases; for central Illinois it must be "No" in most cases. As it turned out, Lincoln's answers were in line with what the trend of his thought up to this point would lead one to expect. He gave his answers at Freeport, on the occasion of the second debate. He said boldly that, in answer to Question 6, he was implicitly, if not expressly, pledged to a belief in the right and duty of Congress to prohibit slavery in all the United States Territories. He did not wish to see slavery extended. For the rest of the questions, he answered in general "No." He was not pledged in the directions which Douglas asked. But he added that, though not pledged, he had his hopes and opinions. He thought the Southern states were entitled to a Congressional fugitive slave law. He confessed frankly that he would be glad to know that no more slave states were to enter the Union, but he thought that if a Territory, having prevented slavery within its borders, should then come none the less to set up a slave constitution when the time came for them to be admitted as a state into the Union, he would feel obliged to admit them. On the matter of slavery in the District of Columbia, he said once more that he would be glad to see it go, but he reiterated the principles he had advocated in his bill as a Congressman—abolition should be gradual, it should be accepted by a majority of the qualified voters in the District and it should be accompanied by compensation. The abolition of the slave trade between the states was a problem on which, as he had said, he was not pledged, and he added that if it should be found that Congress had power to abolish it, he would still not be in favour of the exercise of the power "unless upon some conservative principle as I conceive it, akin to what I have said in relation to the abolition of slavery in the District of Columbia."

In these answers Lincoln shows his familiar method of thought. He is opposed to the extension of slavery and he wishes to see the United States all free. But he proposes no extreme methods to reach the extreme goal. His methods are moderate; he prefers to adopt "some conservative principle" where others advocated abolitionism. His answers go as far as he can to reassure central and southern Illinois, but his bold statement of his immediate programme in relation to the Territories and of his ultimate goal of a free Union must necessarily confirm the extreme pro-slavery men in their hostility to him. That was inevitable. No honest man could expect otherwise.

So far Douglas had had his turn at interrogation. At Freeport Lincoln, having answered Douglas's questions, now put to Douglas four questions addressed particularly to the doctrine of popular sovereignty. This is the second aspect of the debates to which attention must be given. One of the four questions was:

"Can the people of a United States Territory, in any lawful way, against the wish of any citizen of the United States, exclude slavery from its limits prior to the formation of a state constitution?"

This was a difficult question for Douglas. If he said that the people of a Territory could not exclude slavery, he was accepting the Dred Scott decision; he was admitting that popular sovereignty was valueless and he was giving away to the Republicans and to Lincoln the whole case he had built up in favour of popular sovereignty as a means by which in practice the North could prevent the extension of slavery. If he said that the people of a Territory could exclude slavery, he was repudiating the Dred Scott decision and saying to the South that, in spite of that decision, slavery could not spread; the Territories could be denied to Southern control.

The answer Douglas gave was an extension of that which he had outlined in his speech at Springfield in June 1857 after the Dred Scott decision. He said:

"It matters not what way the Supreme Court may hereafter decide as to the abstract question whether slavery may or may not go into a Territory under the Constitution, the people have the lawful means to introduce it or exclude it as they please, for the reason that slavery cannot exist a day or an hour anywhere unless it is supported by local police regulations. These police regulations can be established by the local legislature, and if the people are opposed to slavery they will elect representatives to that body who will by unfriendly legislation effectually prevent the introduction of it into their midst. If, on the contrary, they are for it, then legislation will favour its extension."

This answer meant that the Dred Scott decision could be nullified by the failure of a Territorial legislature to protect the rights of the slave-owner. It was an answer which did Douglas great harm with the Southern members of his party. This "Freeport Doctrine," as it came to be called, coupled with his quarrel with President Buchanan and the party leaders over the Lecompton Constitution, made Douglas many enemies in his party. It meant that when, in 1860, the Democratic party had to choose a candidate for the Presidency, Douglas, who might otherwise have been nominated unanimously, came forward as a nominee of a section only of the party. It is a reasonable conjecture that the Freeport Doctrine and Popular Sovereignty lost Douglas the Presidency in 1860.

Meanwhile it won him the election for Senator in Illinois. Although Lincoln made the most of Douglas's answer in southern Illinois, particularly in the third debate at Jonesboro, well in the south in a part of Illinois called "Egypt," the Freeport Doctrine appealed to enough people in central and northern Illinois to secure Douglas's election. Lincoln had foreseen this consequence of his question. His supporters had urged him not to put the question. "If you do," they said, "you can never be Senator." "Gentlemen," Lincoln said, "I am killing larger game; if Douglas answers, he can never be President and the battle of 1860 is worth a hundred of this." Lincoln did not mean that he was putting the question in order that he himself might become President. Whatever his ambitions, there was no reason yet for him to think that he would be the Republican candidate. All that he meant was that he was out to split the Democratic party in the Presidential election and so secure the election of a Republican.

But Lincoln's opposition to Douglas over popular sovereignty went deeper than a question of tactics. Here is the third feature of the debates which deserves mention. Lincoln and Douglas were at one in desiring the preservation of the Union; they both put the Union first. But whereas Douglas was prepared to say that he did not mind whether the Union was free or slave, Lincoln said boldly that he wanted the Union to be all free. And he based himself here on a deep moral issue. Slavery was a wrong. In his reply to Douglas in the seventh and last debate at Alton, he put this point:

"The real issue in this controversy—the one pressing upon every mind—is the sentiment on the part of one class who looks upon the institution of slavery as a wrong, and of another class that does not look upon it as a wrong. The sentiment that contemplates the institution of slavery in this country as a wrong is the sentiment of the Republican party. . . . They look upon it as being a moral, social and political wrong; and while they contemplate it as such, they nevertheless have due regard for its actual existence among us, and the difficulties of getting rid of it in any satisfactory way, and to all the constitutional obligations thrown about it. Yet having a due regard for these, they desire a policy in regard to it that looks to its not creating any more danger. They insist that it, as far as may be, be treated as a wrong, and one of the methods of treating it as a wrong is to make provision that it shall grow no larger. They also desire a policy that looks to a peaceful end of slavery some time, as being a wrong. . . . If there be a man amongst us who does not think that the institution of slavery is wrong in any one of the aspects of which I have spoken, he is misplaced and ought not to be with us. And if there be a man amongst us who is so impatient of it as a wrong as to disregard its actual presence among us and the difficulty of getting rid of it suddenly in a satisfactory way, and to disregard the constitutional obligations thrown about it, that man is misplaced if he is on our platform. We disclaim sympathy with him in practical action. He is not placed properly with us. . . .

"On the other hand, I have said there is a sentiment which treats it as not being wrong. That is the Democratic sentiment of this day. I do not mean to say that every man who stands within that range positively asserts that it is right. That class will include all who positively assert that it is right, and all who, like Judge Douglas, treat it as indifferent, and do not say it is either right or wrong. . . . He contends that whatever community wants slaves has a right to have them. So they have if it is not a wrong. But if it is a wrong, he cannot say people have a right to do wrong."

So the two were divided on this issue. Lincoln had taken his stand on a moral ground; he had taken his choice between tolerating a slave Union and advocating a free Union. Douglas evaded or postponed the choice. And for the time being he succeeded. On November 2, 1858, the state elections were held in Illinois.[3] The Democrats still retained a majority in the legislature, although the Republicans made some gains. There had been some doubt how far the Democrats would be united in supporting Douglas after his breach with the party in Washington and his statement of the Freeport Doctrine. But when the election was held on January 5, 1859, Douglas was returned by fifty-four votes to forty-six recorded for Lincoln.

The contest of principles did not end with the election of Douglas. Lincoln went on to speak in other states, asserting everywhere his doctrine that slavery must not be extended because slavery was a wrong, and that no policy short of that could be sufficient for the Republican party. In December he

[3] Senators at this time and until 1913 were not directly elected by the people of a state; they were elected by the legislature of the state. Strictly speaking, the campaign in which Lincoln and Douglas were speaking was the election campaign for the state legislature of Illinois.

undertook a tour in Kansas. He was now becoming a national figure. His contest with Douglas had brought him on to the national stage. On February 27, 1860, he addressed a great meeting at the Cooper Institute in New York, and stated once more and with great effect the opinions he had slowly worked out in the preceding years.

The excitement and heat of the contest at this crisis in the history of the United States was suddenly inflamed once more by an incident in October 1859, an incident which was comparable in its effect on the South with the beating of Senator Sumner by Preston Brooks in its effect on the North. On the night of Sunday, October 16, John Brown, the anti-slavery fanatic whose murderous attack at Potawotomie in Kansas in May 1856 had gone unpunished, suddenly attacked an arsenal of the United States situated at Harper's Ferry in Virginia. John Brown was at the head of a little band of thirteen whites, including three of his sons, and five negroes, and he seems to have intended that his raid should help to free the slaves and found for them a refuge in the Appalachian mountains. After fierce fighting John Brown was captured on Tuesday, October 18, but only after the militia had been called out and with them a detachment of United States marines under the command of Robert E. Lee, later to be a great general in the Civil War. John Brown was tried for murder and treason, condemned to death and hanged on December 2. His last speech was dignified and fervent, and many opponents of slavery in the North regarded him thenceforth as a martyr in the cause. They were to sing:

> "John Brown's body lies a-mould'ring in his
>   grave
>   But his soul goes marching on."

To the South he had been the dreadful portent of a negro rising, the most fearful event the slave states could imagine. Despite the condemnation of John Brown's raid which was expressed by parties and politicians of the North, the South saw in the event a sign of what must be expected of "Black Republicanism."

Lincoln said of John Brown's raid: "It was not a slave

insurrection. It was an attempt by white men to get up a revolt among slaves, in which the slaves refused to participate. In fact it was so absurd that the slaves, with all their ignorance, saw plainly enough that it could not succeed."

Chapter 6

Presidential Candidate and President-elect

"This Lincoln, President now by the grace of luck,
Disunion, politics, Douglas and a few speeches. . . ."
STEPHEN VINCENT BENÉT: *John Brown's Body*.

THE STRUGGLE BETWEEN North and South now became intense, as the year 1860 brought round again the time for a Presidential election. For the South the contest seemed to be a matter of life and death. With the admission of Minnesota and Oregon to the Union in 1858 and 1859 as free states, the totals were now eighteen free states and fifteen slave states. The South were in a minority; and it was difficult to see how they could ever become a majority or even maintain an equality. Since 1845, when Texas was admitted as a slave state, five new states had been admitted to the Union, and all of them had come in as free states—Iowa in 1846, Wisconsin in 1848, California in 1850 and Minnesota and Oregon. At some time New Mexico and even Arizona might be admitted as states where slavery was legal, but that marked the limit of what the South might hope to gain.

And now the Republican party had come into the field and Lincoln stood pledged to the prevention of the spread of slavery into the Territories, and he spoke of slavery as a "wrong." For the South their choice came to this. Either they must control the government of the Union, in spite of their inferior position, or they must leave the Union and form a new Union among themselves, organised upon their own principles. Now, there was only one way in which the South could control the government of the Union, and that was through the Democratic party. The Democratic party was not a sectional party. It had supporters in the North and the South, and if it remained united it had a chance of obtaining the Presidency. The South predominated in the Democratic party and therefore could control its administration. Here was the opportunity. But if the Democratic party should lose the Presidency, if the Republicans, the party of the North, should win, then the South would have lost their influence. They might as well leave the Union at once.

So it was that, when the Presidential campaign came on in 1860, the South declared that if a Republican was elected to the Presidency, they would secede from the Union. This did not mean that the South proposed a civil war if the Republicans should win. They anticipated evidently a peaceful secession. But they were convinced that if the Republicans gained control, the South would be better out of the Union than in it. The maintenance of the Union depended in 1860, therefore, on the victory of the Democratic party, for only through that party could the South gain control over the government of the United States. Such was the position as the parties proceeded in 1860 to the choice of their candidates for the Presidency.

But now the fatal thing happened. The Democratic party split on the slavery question, and with the split they lost the Presidency. On April 23, 1860, the convention of the Democratic party met at Charleston, in South Carolina, to select their candidate and to frame a platform. Douglas was the obvious candidate. He was a Northern Senator, from Illinois, a free state. He could be expected to carry some states in the North and West, and these with a solid support from the Southern states might have given the Democrats a victory. The Union would have been preserved—not a single state, save possibly South Carolina, would have seceded. But the Southern states would not give this solid support to Douglas. They believed that he had deceived them. His doctrine of popular sovereignty had seemed to offer a promise that slavery could be protected in the Territories, but now his attitude over the Lecompton Constitution for Kansas in Congress and his Freeport Doctrine, which positively encouraged and instructed Territories in the methods of evading the constitutional guarantees of slavery, made him unacceptable to the South. Yet Douglas was the one candidate of the Democratic party who might have carried the election.[1] With his rejection the election was certainly lost.

[1] Whether, in fact, he would have done so is, of course, a matter of speculation. See below, p. 86.

Yet it could hardly have been otherwise when the temper of the South is considered. The South had come to the conclusion that no compromise on the rights and wrongs of slavery could be tolerated. Here they took up the same position as Lincoln. No one could be indifferent on the question. Lincoln urged the Republicans to reject Douglas and his popular sovereignty because slavery was a wrong; it was not right or wrong, as Douglas maintained. The South demanded that the Democrats reject Douglas and his popular sovereignty because they believed that slavery was right, and not right or wrong, as Douglas maintained. In the convention at Charleston, William Yancey, of Alabama, demanded that the Democratic party should say openly "that slavery was right." The Democratic Senator Pugh, of Ohio, a Northern free state, said: "Gentlemen of the South, you mistake us— you mistake us—we will not do it." And so, on April 30, after a week's deliberations, the delegates from the cotton states of the South walked out of the Democratic convention and the party had split.

It was not possible for those who remained in the convention to nominate Douglas, because under the rules of the Democratic party (until 1936) it was necessary for a candidate to receive the support of a two-thirds majority of the delegates. The convention therefore adjourned to meet at Baltimore. After many confusing manœuvres, with further withdrawals and returns, on June 18 the convention chose Douglas as the official candidate of the Democratic party. Those who had withdrawn then held a separate convention of their own in Baltimore (and there was another going on at Richmond in ambiguous relations with it), and on June 28 nominated the then Vice-President, John C. Breckinridge, of Kentucky, as their candidate. Their programme was the extension of slavery and the annexation of Cuba, where a further development of Southern economy was hoped for.

While the Democratic party was undergoing these crises, the Republicans were making their choice. Few would have prophesied that they would pick Abraham Lincoln. He was not the outstanding man in the Republican party. William H. Seward, of New York, and Salmon P. Chase, of Ohio, were its most prominent men and the outstanding candidates.

Seward had been Governor of New York State, and a United States Senator from the state since 1848; Chase had served two terms as Governor of Ohio and had been a United States Senator for six years. But, as often happens in the choice of Presidential candidates in the United States, the prominent men are passed over, for their very prominence means that they will have enemies as well as friends. Seward and Chase were both thought to be radical and extremist on the slavery issue. It was Seward who had spoken of the "irrepressible conflict," yet he was no more extreme than Lincoln. But he was a prominent man, and what he said was not forgotten. Nor do party organisers always welcome a strong man in the White House. They will wish to control him, not to be controlled by him. For this reason the great party leader is not always, or indeed usually, chosen as Presidential candidate in the United States.

Lincoln worked hard to obtain the nomination. His ambition operated here as it had from the beginning. After his speech at the Cooper Institute in New York on February 27, 1860, which made him known in the East, he had undertaken a tour of the New England states. He returned to Springfield in March and set about active negotiations to secure the support of the Illinois delegation to the Republican national convention. The state convention was held in May, and Lincoln carried the meeting. The convention instructed its delegates to support Lincoln at the national convention. An incident in the meeting of the state convention illustrates one factor which was used in favour of Lincoln's nomination and election. John Hanks, a cousin of Lincoln, marched into the convention carrying two fence rails, which he claimed Lincoln and he had split thirty years before on the Sangamon river near Decatur, Illinois, where the convention was then meeting. Here was evidence of the frontier man, the candidate who represented the West and its interests, and who could withstand the pressure of Eastern industrialists and Southern cotton-growers. Lincoln became known as "the rail splitter," and doubtless he gained some support from this.[2]

2 Humorists called his eldest son, Robert, "The Prince of Rails" —a not inappropriate title as it turned out, for he was to become in later life an executive of the Pullman Company.

The Republican national convention met at Chicago, in a "wigwam" specially constructed for the purpose. It proceeded to its solemn task with the combination of intrigue, foolery, bellowing, shouting, hissing, conviviality, farce, melodrama and other forms of that reckless tempting of Providence which characterise these gatherings in the United States. What the convention wanted was a candidate who could counter all the influence of Douglas in the Northern states. They could not hope to carry the cotton states, of course, but if they could win such states as New Jersey, Pennsylvania, Indiana and Illinois from Douglas, they would have a chance of snatching success from the Democrats. Lincoln had shown himself the man who could stand up to Douglas, and his debates in 1858 and the tenacity with which he pursued the arguments against popular sovereignty marked him out as a good candidate.

The convention spent its first two days adopting a platform while bargaining went on behind the scenes. On the third day it came to a ballot. An absolute majority was needed for a candidate to be chosen—that is to say, more than all the other candidates put together—but there was no requirement of a two-thirds majority, as in the Democratic party. Voting was by delegations from states, each state being given a voting power roughly proportionate to its population. Sometimes a state's delegation was not unanimous and a fraction of its vote might be cast for a candidate. With these preliminaries in mind we can understand the proceedings in the "wigwam." On the first ballot Seward led with 173½ votes; Lincoln had 102. On the second ballot Seward had 184½ and Lincoln 181. On the third ballot Lincoln was chosen. The date was May 18, 1860, less than a month after the Democratic party had split upon the choice of Douglas at its convention in Charleston, but before the choices of Douglas and Breckinridge had been made. Lincoln's nomination was not secured without some hard bargaining. Between the first and second ballots Lincoln's managers promised the supporters of Simon Cameron, who controlled the party machine in his state of Pennsylvania and who was a candidate for nomination, that if they transferred their support to Lincoln, Cameron should be given Cabinet office if Lincoln was elected. This was a promise which Lincoln had forbidden them to make. But he felt obliged to keep to it, and it caused him great trouble in the early years of his administration.

So Lincoln was chosen. And, "if we can put aside the illusion which besets us, who read the preceding history, if at all, in the light of Lincoln's speeches, and to whom his competitors are mere names, this was the most surprising nomination ever made in America." These are the words of Lincoln's biographer, Lord Charnwood. And he goes on to remark that in rejecting Seward because he was thought to be too radical and in choosing Lincoln, whose words were more extreme than Seward's, but less well known, the convention "to please those who liked compromise, . . . rejected a man who would certainly have compromised, and chose one who would give all that moderation demanded and die before he yielded one further inch." ". . . At this critical moment the fit man was chosen on the very ground of his supposed unfitness."

Lincoln received the news of his nomination at Springfield. He is reported to have said: "Well, gentlemen, there is a little short woman at our house who is probably more interested in this dispatch than I am; and, if you will excuse me, I will take it up and let her see it." On May 19, 1860, he received a delegation from the convention charged with the duty of acquainting him formally with its decision. They came to his house, and after some pleasant conversation he astonished and disappointed some of the party enthusiasts by offering them a glass of water to celebrate the occasion. Lincoln drank no spirits or wines, and he did not smoke. It was a check on conviviality as ordinarily understood and practised in political circles of that day.

To the three candidates already mentioned, there was to be added a fourth. On May 9, the day on which the Illinois Republicans had held their state convention at Decatur and had decided to support Lincoln, there had met, also in Baltimore, the convention of a new party, the Constitutional Union party. Its programme was "the Constitution of the Country, the Union of the States and the enforcement of the laws." It proposed to ignore the question of slavery. It was composed of the conservative members of most parties, who desired to avoid extremes and who saw safety for the Union in an attempt to ignore the issue which so violently divided the other parties. The Constitutional Union nominated John Bell, a Senator from Tennessee, for the Presidency.

Here, then, were the four parties. The Republicans were opposed to the extension of slavery into the Territories, although they advocated no interference with slavery in the states. But they had other ideas. They had their eye on the frontier. They promised settlers a free quarter-section of public land. They remembered also those, like the iron-masters of Pennsylvania and the wool-growers of Ohio, who had suffered from competition with British imports, and they promised a protective tariff. There were thus linked together the industrialism of the North, anti-slavery sentiment and the agricultural vote of the West. This was the party which nominated Lincoln for President and Hannibal Hamlin of Maine for Vice-President. The Douglas Democrats professed indifference on the question of slavery and proposed to leave it to the people of the Territories to decide whether they accepted it or not. The Breckinridge Democrats—who were supported by President Buchanan—declared that slavery was right and that its extension and protection should be sought. And finally there was the Constitutional Union party, with John Bell attempting not merely indifference to but ignorance of the slavery issue.

In the campaign itself Lincoln took no part. He remained at Springfield and left the conduct of the struggle to his party organisations in the various states. He wrote a friendly note to Hannibal Hamlin, the Vice-Presidential candidate whom he had never seen. He received many callers. One thing he did at this time inevitably interests the student of his life. He grew a beard. Most people think of Lincoln as a man with a short beard and assume maybe that he had it all his adult life. In fact he grew it at the age of fifty-one, after he became a Presidential candidate. In October 1860 he received a letter from a little girl in Westfield, New York, called Grace Bedell, who suggested that he should grow a beard so that he might look more dignified when he became President. He appears to have been influenced by this suggestion. He let his beard grow. And when the train carrying him to Washington as President-elect in March 1861 stopped at Westfield, Lincoln asked for Grace Bedell. She was brought to the train and Lincoln kissed her. He was no longer the clean-shaven politician familiar to Illinois.

Before giving the figures of the result in the Presidential election of November 6, 1860, it is worth noting the method by which the vote is taken. The vote is taken by states: it is not a national vote. Moreover, it is not a direct vote for the Presidential candidates, but a vote by the people of the states[3] for electors who, meeting in their respective states as electoral colleges, are to choose the President. Now, the consequences of this method of election need to be considered. If in any state a majority of the voters chose electors pledged to support Lincoln, for example, then all the votes cast for other electors were wasted. Lincoln would carry all the Presidential electors for that state. And similarly in the case of the other candidates. It might thus happen that a Presidential candidate might have many thousands of votes cast for him and yet not obtain a corresponding support in the electoral colleges. The vote of the people and the vote in the electoral colleges were thus frequently out of proportion to each other.

This, in fact, was what happened in the election of 1860. Lincoln polled 1,866,452 votes,[4] Douglas 1,376,957 votes, Breckinridge 849,781 votes and Bell 588,879 votes. But in terms of electors in the electoral colleges the result was different. Lincoln had carried all the free states except New Jersey, where by a party bargain three electors out of the seven to be chosen were for Douglas and four for Lincoln. Yet Douglas had polled heavily in all the states where Lincoln had succeeded. But his votes were of no avail unless he actually carried the poll for the electoral colleges. So in the electoral colleges Lincoln had 180 votes, but Douglas had only twelve—the three from New Jersey and nine from

[3] Except in South Carolina, where, in 1860, electors were still chosen by the legislature of the state.

[4] Lincoln went to the poll himself. He had usually voted for himself in the past, but he did not do so on this occasion. He abstained from voting for the Presidential electors, but voted for the other offices which were also contested at the same poll.

Missouri, the only state which he actually won. Breckinridge had obtained his votes only in the South, and in particular he carried all the cotton states, and in addition North Carolina, Delaware and Maryland. He had seventy-two votes in the electoral colleges. But he had not carried the whole South. Bell carried three Southern states—Virginia, Kentucky and Tennessee—and he had thirty-nine votes in the electoral colleges.

It can be seen from this vote also, that although Lincoln had more "popular" votes—that is to say, votes by the people —than any single one of his opponents, if all the opposition votes had been put together he was in a minority of about a million, and that, too, in a total popular vote of a little over four and a half million. The majority of the American people did not vote for Lincoln. Whether they would have done so had there been only one candidate in opposition to him, and that one Douglas, cannot be known for certain. It is possible that they would not. If the Democratic party could have united on Douglas, they might well have obtained a majority of the popular vote. Even so, it is not certain that this would have meant also a majority for Douglas in the electoral colleges. On the actual vote that took place an estimate has been made of what the result would have been if all the votes cast for Lincoln's three opponents had been concentrated on a single one. Clearly there would have been a popular majority for Lincoln's opponent, but it is calculated that Lincoln would still have carried the electoral colleges by a majority of thirty-five votes. That is a calculation based upon the vote actually cast. But had there been only the one candidate, Douglas, in opposition to Lincoln, it is not certain how, in fact, the popular vote would have gone. The speculation is not very profitable. The main point is that Lincoln, like some other American Presidents, was elected by a strong majority in the electoral colleges, although on the popular vote more votes were cast for all his opponents put together than for himself. And in that respect Lincoln resembles more than one British Prime Minister. It is a consequence of electoral systems where a simple majority is held to be decisive and where proportional representation does not prevail.

So Abraham Lincoln was elected President of the United

States on November 6, 1860. But another provision of the Constitution of the United States now affects the situation. Until 1933 the President of the United States, although elected in November, did not take office until the following March.[5] This meant that there might elapse a period of months in which a defeated administration and a defeated Congress continued in office, while the newly elected President and Congress were powerless to take any hand in the control of affairs. Sometimes the interval has not been harmful to the United States, and obviously not so when a President has been re-elected for a second term. But at other times it has caused a serious worsening in the political situation. This happened when the Republican President Hoover was defeated by the Democrat Franklin Roosevelt in November 1932. An economic crisis had fallen upon the United States, and nobody had authority sufficient to control it. It happened also when the Democrats were defeated by the Republicans in November 1860, and Abraham Lincoln was obliged to stand by powerless while President Buchanan and the Democratic party, already divided within itself, continued to hold office in Washington. In that interval critical events occurred in the history of the American Union.

It had been made clear by some of the Southern states that if a Republican President was elected, they would leave the Union.[6] The Governor of South Carolina had communicated privately with the governors of other Southern states in October, before the election was held, to discover what support South Carolina would get if it seceded. The answers were encouraging. Accordingly, when the election of Lincoln was certain, the legislature of South Carolina called a convention in the state to consider the state's relationship to the government of the United States. On December 20, 1860, the convention, meeting at Charleston, unanimously declared "that the Union now subsisting between South Carolina and other states under the name of 'The United States of America' is hereby dissolved."

[5] By the Twentieth Amendment of 1933 he now takes office in January.

[6] Not a single vote was cast for Lincoln in any of the states that seceded except Virginia.

The lead of South Carolina was quickly followed. Not that all the cotton states were unanimous. A powerful minority in favour of the Union existed in most of them, and some leaders, like Jefferson Davis, of Mississippi, thought that action should be postponed until Lincoln's administration had been given a trial. But a strong movement for secession became predominant. By February 1, 1861, six more states had seceded—Mississippi on January 9, Florida on January 10, Alabama on January 11, Georgia on January 19, Louisiana on January 26 and Texas on February 1. On February 4 delegates from all these states, except Texas, met in Congress at Montgomery, Alabama, and on February 8 they formed the Confederate States of America, choosing Jefferson Davis as their provisional President and Alexander H. Stephens, of Georgia, as their provisional Vice-President. In March they had adopted a permanent constitution, which was to take effect in the next year. Such was the situation which confronted Abraham Lincoln by the time that he was inaugurated as President in March 1861.

But that was not all. While these seven cotton states of the South had taken these steps, no effective action had been taken against them by the Buchanan administration. As states seceded, their Senators and Representatives withdrew from Congress at Washington; their citizens began withdrawal from the Army of the United States. In each seceded state the state government took possession of the Federal arsenals, customs houses and post offices. Some preparations were made by the states for possible military action. In the end only Fort Sumter in the harbour of Charleston, Fort Pickens in Pensacola Bay and the fortifications at Key West remained in the hands of the government of the United States. But President Buchanan took no action. He was advised by his Attorney-General that secession was illegal, but that he had no right to coerce a seceding state. He therefore condemned secession, and he urged compromise and peaceful settlement. But he never spoke to the seceded states as President Andrew Jackson spoke to South Carolina in 1832, when that state had passed an ordinance to nullify the tariff act of Congress. Then Jackson had said that it was his duty to see that the laws of the United States were enforced and that he would do it, and that disunion by armed force was treason, and those who attempted it must suffer the consequences of treason. This was the way in which a Democratic President, famous for his belief in the need to protect the rights of the states, had spoken, and on this basis had he negotiated a compromise with South Carolina which avoided secession. But President Buchanan spoke no such language now.

Nor did Congress, in which, before secession had begun to take effect, the Democrats still retained a majority, give any positive lead. The withdrawal of the Senators from the seceding states gave the Republicans a majority in the Senate. An act was passed to admit Kansas to the Union under her latest free constitution, thus endorsing Douglas in his confidence in popular sovereignty in this case at any rate. The Territories of Nevada, Colorado and Dakota were organised, with no mention of slavery. A tariff act, the Morrill Act, the first strongly protective tariff since the controversy of 1832, in which Jackson had intervened, was also passed. Its passage could have been prevented had the Southern Senators been present. These were the measures with which Congress was concerned. The great issues of secession and slavery were not dealt with.

Not that attempts at compromise were wanting. There was one attempt, known as the Crittenden Compromise, which deserves attention. On December 18, 1860, Senator Crittenden proposed a constitutional amendment which would provide for the re-establishment of the Missouri Compromise line of 36° 30' as the division between slavery and freedom in the Territories, with the positive establishment of slavery in the Territories south of that line; for non-interference by Congress with slavery in the states and in the District of Columbia; and for compensation to the owners of fugitive slaves who were not recovered. So far as Lincoln was concerned, his attitude to this compromise was in accordance with his policy as publicly expounded and as developed over a long period. He was prepared to accept the second and third points, if the Southern Senators would appeal to their states against secession, but he could not accept the first point, which involved the principle of extending and guaranteeing the extension of slavery into the Territories. The Crittenden Compromise came to nothing. In the succeeding weeks the seven Southern states seceded. And when, on February 4, a Peace Convention met at Washington, at the suggestion of Virginia, the seceding states showed their interest in it by meeting on that same date at Montgomery to prepare for the establishment of the Confederate States of America.

Chapter 7

The War

"And yet—what happened to men in war,
Why were they all going out to war?"
STEPHEN VINCENT BENÉT: *John Brown's Body*.

ABRAHAM LINCOLN was sworn in as President of the United States on March 4, 1861. The oath was administered by Chief Justice Taney, who had delivered the opinion of the Supreme Court in the Dred Scott case just four years previously. Standing behind Lincoln was Stephen A. Douglas. When Lincoln fumbled with his silk hat, not quite knowing what to do with it as he prepared to give his Inaugural Address, Douglas took it from him and held it while he spoke. The old enemy was standing by to help. It was symbolic of his attitude in this crisis of the Union. Indeed, it proved to be almost all that he could do, for a few months later, on June 3, he died suddenly in Chicago.

In his Inaugural Address Lincoln used words which resembled closely those of President Andrew Jackson's proclamation to the people of South Carolina in 1832. Addressing the South, he said: "In *your* hands, my dissatisfied fellow-countrymen, and not in *mine*, is the momentous issue of civil war. The government will not assail *you*. I hold, that in contemplation of universal law and of the Constitution, the Union of these states is perpetual. . . . No state, upon its own mere motion can lawfully get out of the Union. . . . I shall take care, as the Constitution itself expressly enjoins upon me, that the laws of the Union be faithfully executed in all the states. . . . The power confided to me will be used to hold, occupy and possess the property and places belonging to the government, and to collect the duties and imposts."

The first test of these words was provided by the situation of two forts—Fort Pickens at Pensacola, Florida, on the Gulf of Mexico, and Fort Sumter in Charleston Harbour, South Carolina. They had not yet fallen into the hands of the seceding states, but their retention by the United States could not continue indefinitely unless they were reinforced and supplied. But any attempt so to assist them would be regarded as a hostile act by the seceding states and might be expected to lead to war. President Buchanan had taken no action. The problem was ticklish. After all, if the seceding states might yet be brought back to the Union, surely nothing should be done to irritate them, especially when the forts concerned were of no strategic importance to the Union government in coercing the states. They were symbolic only. If an attempt was made to supply them, that attempt would be a symbol of the determination of the President to maintain the laws of the Union.

But more was involved than the risk of annoying the seceded states. It must be emphasised that up to this point only seven states had seceded, the cotton states of the lower South. The South as a whole had not seceded, and there was good hope that the states of the upper South might be kept within the Union. After all, in the Presidential election, Virginia, Kentucky and Tennessee had shown majorities for Bell, the candidate of Constitutional Union; they had rejected secession. Virginia was of particular importance, for its territory extended round the boundaries of Pennsylvania to a point within a hundred miles of Lake Erie and could provide the base for an advance which would cut off one half of the North from the other. Further, if Virginia went, other states would follow. Maryland might go, and Maryland and Virginia between them surrounded Washington, so that if both seceded, the capital was lost. So Lincoln too had to proceed with caution in deciding what action he should take about supplying the forts.

Fort Sumter provided the test. Major Anderson, who commanded the fort, notified the War Department that his supplies were running out and he must receive reinforcements and supplies if he was to hold on. Lincoln finally took the decision, towards the end of March, to send a relief expedition, with provisions only, to Fort Sumter and to Fort Pickens, and he told the Confederate authorities of his intention. Five out of seven members of his Cabinet opposed the decision and his military adviser was against it. His Secretary of State, William H. Seward, his rival for the Republican nomination, attempted to dissuade him by a counter-plan; indeed, he had already given representatives of the South to understand that Sumter would be evacuated; and he even went so far as to secure, by deception, the diversion of the capital ship of the Sumter expedition to accompany the expedition to Fort Pickens.

The relief expedition was ordered to sail on April 6. On the night of April 11–12 Confederate officers arrived at Fort Sumter and called on Major Anderson to surrender. Anderson did not like the idea of civil war, but he felt he ought to make some show of doing his duty. No word of the relief expedition had reached him, so he proposed to the Confederate officers that he should surrender in two days' time, when his supplies would be exhausted, provided he received "no controlling instructions from his government or additional supplies." They refused this offer and gave orders for the fort to be fired on. This action had not been authorised by President Jefferson Davis. He had expressly ordered the general commanding the Charleston District not to fire upon Fort Sumter unless it was absolutely necessary in order to prevent reinforcement. None the less, at 4:30 a.m. on Apirl 12 the first shots in the Civil War were fired. The relief expedition appeared, to provision, not to reinforce, but it could not pass the guns, for its capital ship had been diverted. On April 13 Major Anderson accepted terms of surrender, and the garrison marched out on April 14.

President Lincoln acted instantly. On April 15 he called for 75,000 volunteers to put down combinations "too powerful to be suppressed by the ordinary course of judicial proceedings," and "to cause the laws to be duly executed," and he called Congress to a special session for July 4. In so acting he received the full and public support of Douglas, whose last days were devoted to the support of Lincoln in the exercise of all his constitutional functions to preserve the Union. Lincoln's actions over the Sumter affair have been much discussed. Some think he was provoking a war; others that he found events too much for him and stumbled into war; others that by patience and fair dealing he had first exhausted all that diplomacy could do and finally resorted to war. The truth probably is that Lincoln's motives were honourable and his purpose firm and just; but there were also ill-luck and mismanagement against him. But Douglas, his old enemy, at any rate, supported him. Lincoln's action meant, as he knew it must, that Virginia and other Southern states would secede. Two days after Lincoln's proclamation Virginia seceded, and it was a grievous blow. A few months later, however, West Virginia, of great strategic importance to the North, declared its indepedence of the rest of the state and came over to the side of the Union. It became a separate state of the Union in 1863. But it gave little aid to the Union, and it seems clear that its breach with the rest of Virginia was due more to its hatred of the planter aristocracy than to enthusiasm for the Union.

Three more Southern states followed Virginia—Arkansas on May 6, North Carolina on May 21 and Tennessee on June 8. There was an anxious time with Maryland. Its legislature protested against Lincoln's coercion of the South, but it went no further. Kentucky, too, protested and refused at first. It was not until the end of 1861 that it finally came to the Union side. Missouri has been described as "practically under a dual régime throughout the war." Delaware remained loyal to the Union. Finally California, after a struggle, adopted the side of the Union, but it was so far removed from the rest of the Union that it could give no aid to the Union cause except in money. And so the sides were taken. It was not, as will be seen, a war between the free states and the slave states, but between the free states and four border states on the one side, and eleven seceded slave states on the other, although the four border states could not be counted upon with certainty. They contributed their quota of men to both sides, probably as many to the Confederacy as to the Union, and Lincoln's policy had always to be framed with an eye to retaining their allegiance.

What was the war about? Historians have given many answers, and it is difficult to say in a short space sufficient to justify an answer in the light of the varied explanations that have been put forward. But the war itself was fought in order to decide whether the United States should continue. The North fought in order to prevent the South from seceding; the South fought in order to secede. That was the immediate cause. But why did the South wish to secede? Upon what question or questions were they irreconcilably opposed to the rest of the Union? Great historical controversies rage about these matters, and the relative importance of the various factors is hotly debated. For some curious reason the cause which appears obviously the most potent to some students—the divergence of opinion upon the institution of slavery—is relegated by others to a subordinate place. Divergence of economic interests, and in particular the clash over tariff policy, is thought more important by some; others describe it as a conflict between two different views about the rights of the states within the Union under the Constitution—whether the states were sovereign bodies free to secede if they chose, or whether they were indissolubly linked in the Union.

In the view of the present writer there is no doubt that slavery was the overwhelmingly predominant cause of the break-up in the Union so far as the states of the lower South were concerned, and it was the one issue upon which the North found itself unable to compromise. Tariff protection and state rights had some place in assisting the division, but of these two, tariff protection seems the less important. State rights operated upon the states of the upper South after Lincoln's proclamation of April 15. Many people there believed that it was contrary to the true nature of the Constitution that a state should be coerced once it had chosen, through the due forms of a convention of the people, to secede. They preferred to leave the Union if, after all, a contrary interpretation of the Constitution was to prevail. Yet it must be stressed that this invocation of state rights for the most part arose from the divergence upon the issue of slavery. It was the denial of rights about slavery which led to the claim to secede. At the bottom of all these differences lay the fundamental divergence between two societies, one based upon slavery and the other opposed to it. Lincoln himself, speaking to a delegation of negroes in August 1862, said: "But for your race among us, there could not be war, although many men engaged on either side do not care for you one way or the other."

This analysis of the causes of secession, and thus of the war, seems to be supported by the speeches of Jefferson Davis, the President of the Confederacy, and Alexander Stephens, the Vice-President, at the very outset of secession and civil war. Stephens lays the greater emphasis on slavery. "The new Constitution," he said, "has put at rest for ever all the agitating questions relating to our peculiar institution, African slavery as its exists amongst us, the proper status of the negro in our form of civilisation. This was the immediate cause of the late rupture and present revolution. . . . Most of the leading statesmen at the time of the formation of the old Constitution were [of opinion] that the enslavement of the African was in violation of the laws of nature; that it was wrong in principle, socially, morally and politically. . . . Those ideas, however, were fundamentally wrong. They rested upon the assumption of the equality of races. This was an error. It was a sandy foundation, and the government built upon it fell when 'the storm came and the wind blew.' Our new government is founded upon exactly the opposite idea; its foundations are laid, its corner-stone rests, upon the truth that the negro is not equal to the white man, that slavery—subordination to the superior race—is his natural and normal condition."

Jefferson Davis in his first message to the Confederate Congress narrated the steps which led to secession, and his account lays less stress upon slavery. He speaks of the perversion of the original meaning of the Constitution, by which "an organisation created by the states to secure the blessings of liberty and independence against *foreign* aggression has been gradually perverted into a machine for their control in their *domestic* affairs." But even here, although the Northern states are charged with an attempt to interfere with the economic life of the Southern states "by imposing burdens on commerce as a protection to their manufacturing and shipping interests," the interference in domestic affairs which was most feared and hated was the interference, actual or anticipated, with the institution of slavery.

Jefferson Davis went on: "In addition to the long-continued and deep-seated resentment felt by the Southern states at the persistent abuse of the powers they had delegated to the Congress, for the purpose of enriching the manufacturing and shipping classes of the North at the expense of the

South, there has existed for nearly half a century another subject of discord, involving interests of such transcendent magnitude as at all times to create the apprehension in the minds of many devoted lovers of the Union that its permanence was impossible." And he goes on to describe how, in the mind of the Southern states, a series of steps had been taken in the North for the purpose of rendering insecure the tenure of property in slaves, culminating in the election as President of a man belonging to a party whose avowed objects would result in "rendering the property in slaves so insecure as to be comparatively worthless, and thereby annihilating in effect property worth thousands of millions of dollars." With interests of such overwhelming magnitude imperilled, the people of the Southern states were driven by the conduct of the North to the adoption of some course of action to prevent the danger with which they were openly menaced.

"On their own showing, then," says S. E. Morison in his *History of the United States*, "the states of the lower South seceded as a result of a long series of dissatisfactions respecting the Northern attitude towards slavery." In the states of the upper South the causes were more mixed. "The motives for this second group of secessions, beginning with Virginia, were obviously very different from those of the lower South. The upper South had been willing to give the Lincoln administration a trial. But it was drawn to the lower South by ties of blood, and the determination to keep that region a 'White man's country.' The emotion was rationalised by the theory of state sovereignty, which was strong and genuine in eastern Virginia and Maryland, and in western and central Tennessee. According to this theory, every state had a right to secede, hence Lincoln's call for coercion was illegal. And it forced the issue; everyone had to choose between defending the Confederacy or helping to put it down."

How were resources distributed between the two sides? In some matters the Union had obvious advantages. In population it was superior to the South: it had about 20,000,-000 free people to the South's 6,000,000 free people and 3,500,000 slaves. How this reflected itself in the numbers of the forces on each side cannot be stated exactly because of certain difficulties in computing the numbers of the two armies. It seems likely that there were about 1,600,000 on the Union side against about 800,000 on the Confederate. Most Southern historians accept the figures of 2,750,000 Union soldiers against 600,000 Confederates. Some guide to the proportion may be obtained from the figures of the census of 1890, which gave 1,034,073 Union veterans and 432,020 Confederates surviving. There is no doubt that in numbers the Union predominated overwhelmingly.

In wealth and industry, too, it far exceeded the South. Until 1863 the South had only one iron works from which to obtain heavy arms and armament—the Tredegar Iron Works in the capital of the Confederacy, Richmond, Virginia. None the less, the South made the very best of what it had. "The Confederacy never lost a battle for want of ammunition," says Morison. The greater part of its equipment had to be imported from Europe, and when, in 1863, the blockade by the Union Navy became effective, the Confederate government had to make use of such resources as had become available in the South by that time. On the whole, the Union armies were better equipped than the Southern, in spite of incompetence in some departments at Washington.

Sea power was on the side of the Union. Though the Navy had been neglected and Congress had refused to vote the money for the building of iron-clads, and though in the early stages of the war the Union Navy-yard at Norfolk, Virginia, had been captured by the Confederates, none the less, by the energy of Lincoln's Secretary of the Navy, Gideon Welles, a naval force was built up to undertake the blockade of the 3,550 miles of coastline from Washington down to the coastal boundary of Texas. But at any rate the Union had a Navy, the South a few ships, and this initial advantage had its effect. Yet in this again the South, by great efforts, improved its position.

One further element favoured the Union. The government of the Union was closer knit, a more integrated institution, than the government of the Confederacy. After all, the states which had seceded had cared more for state sovereignty than for federation, and although they realised that they must be associated together in some way, especially after Fort Sumter, they found it difficult to submit to that degree of subordination which war government requires. No Union general ever had to write, as Lee did of Georgia and Carolina when contemplating an advance: "If these states will give up their troops, I think it can be done." In the same way Jefferson Davis, although a much more experienced politician and administrator than Lincoln, had far greater difficulty in managing the Confederate Congress at Richmond than Lincoln had at Washington. President Davis and his Confederate Congress worked less in harmony than had any President and Congress of the United States since President Tyler's régime of 1841–5. Davis, in four years of office, vetoed thirty-eight bills, all but one of which were passed over his veto. Lincoln in the same period vetoed only three bills.

These are some of the advantages which the Union had over the South. Set against these are certain definite Southern advantages. For a start, the South was on the defensive. It had only to stand firm and wait for the Union to attack, and the Union, to succeed, had to subdue a large empire. The South had the advantage of what strategists call "interior lines"—that is, its communications by road and river ran back behind the front and made movement and reinforcement easy and safe. It is true that the Union had superiority in respect of railways. Not that the South was without railways, but the developments in the North in the ten years before secession had improved communications there much more than in the South. The distances were long, but the trunk lines overcame them.

Then the South had a start over the Union. From the moment of secession they began to prepare for war—not very efficiently at first and not seriously, but they had begun. And after Fort Sumter they went ahead more speedily than the Union. The better military talent was available to them. The ablest officers of the United States Army who were in active service at the time of seccession resigned and joined the Confederacy, many of them after a great moral struggle. There were, among others, Robert E. Lee, Albert S. Johnston, Joseph E. Johnston, J. E. B. Stuart and A. P. Hill. The Union army was bereft of its best men, and it was only after costly experiment that it succeeded in obtaining its leaders and organisers. The greatest of its leaders—generals like Mc-

Clellan, Grant and Sherman—although trained soldiers, who had passed through West Point, the military college of the United States, were all in civil life when the war began. Even when the Union had completed its military organisation, it never caught up with the superiority of the Confederate generals.

The Union was at a further disadvantage in having its capital, Washington, so exposed to the enemy. There it lay on the very borders of Virginia, a rebel state. It stood on the north bank of the Potomac; across the water lay the territory of the Confederacy. The Union set great store upon its capital; it was the symbol of the Union, and, had it been captured, the Confederacy would have gained a great point. Washington was protected by having behind it the state of Maryland, but throughout the war its defence was a major preoccupation with the Union government. "The safety of Washington," says F. L. Paxson in *The American Civil War*, "was the first military problem of the war, and remained among the most difficult to the end." It is true that the Confederate capital itself was established in the state of Virginia, at Richmond, about a hundred miles from Washington as the crow flies, and it was therefore somewhat exposed to attack. The Union regarded its capture as an important priority in its plans. But it was neither so exposed nor so important as Washington. If it were lost, a new capital could have been chosen. Indeed Richmond itself had been selected after an initial period in Montgomery, Alabama, at the outset of the Confederacy; no special tradition or symbolic value was attached to it.

There remains the fact that the South, in social organisation, had an advantage at the outset of the war in that its people took more easily to war; they were more eager for the fight. They could leave their slaves at home to work on the plantations or take them with them as servants and not disturb the basis of their prosperity. For the North no such foundation of labour existed. The recruits who joined the Union armies were free men upon whose labour farms and factories depended. It was only the existence of machines and, in farming, the reaping machine—a newly developed invention—that made it possible for the North to combine raising an army with continuing its agriculture and industry on a sufficient scale.

These were the comparative positions of the opposing sides. The war itself had some unique features. It was the first war in which railways played an important part in communications; it was the first war in which iron-clad ships gave battle to each other. Observation balloons were employed; a kind of submarine was invented. While the war was on, elections for the Congress of the Union had to be held and, in 1864, also a Presidential election. Then, as in 1944, the problems of the soldier's vote were discussed and the process was tried for the first time. Indeed, it is only in 1864 and 1944 that the Presidential election in the United States has occurred in wartime.

Lincoln's work throughout the war—the end of which he survived only by a few days—will be dealt with in detail in the succeeding chapters. It has been thought best to treat his work not chronologically, but rather under the aspects in which his office and policy may be considered—as head of the Union, as Commander-in-Chief, as head of the government, as a leader of the new Republican party, as the emancipator of the slaves and as the planner of post-war reconstruction. For it is with Lincoln and his work that this book is primarily concerned: it does not profess to deal with the course of the Civil War itself. And indeed, since it is said that there were 625 battles and severe skirmishes in the war, it is obvious that space prevents any real discussion of it. But it will be necessary to have the course of the war, in outline at any rate, in the background of one's mind if Lincoln's work is to be understood. It is proposed, therefore, to sketch its main features here before passing to consider Lincoln's work.

The territory of the South, which the Union had to conquer, was divided into three main theatres of war by natural boundaries. There was the eastern theatre, stretching from the coast to the Appalachian mountains. In one part of this theatre the most famous battles were fought—an area bounded by North Carolina, the Appalachian mountains, the Susquehanna river and Chesapeake Bay. The western theatre, which proved to be as important as the eastern, stretched from the Appalachians to the Mississippi. The third theatre lay beyond the Mississippi. Operations in this theatre were of less importance.

In the first year of the war the only important action took place in the eastern theatre. After some months of calling its forces together, the Union took the initiative. The Confederacy had established two armies upon the borders of the Union, one under Joseph E. Johnston, in the Shenandoah Valley, above Harper's Ferry, and the other under Beauregard, on the banks of the Potomac, threatening Washington. Against Beauregard's forces General McDowell advanced with a "grand army" of 30,000 men, crossed the Potomac and advanced towards Manassas Junction in Virginia. There, on July 20, near a small tributary of the Potomac called Bull Run, the two armies met and fought. The Union forces were overcome and retired in a confused rout, but Beauregard did not pursue them—victory had caused confusion in his forces too. It was Bull Run that convinced the Union that a long, hard war lay ahead. Lincoln called General McClellan to Washington the next day and put him in charge of organising a large Union army for the eastern theatre of war. For the rest of the year McClellan, who became General-in-Chief on November 1, systematically built up a large, well-equipped and organised army with the object of striking one crushing and decisive blow upon the Confederates when he was ready. To the annoyance of politicians, and even of Lincoln himself, he refused to do more.

In 1862 McClellan decided at length, and with much pushing from Lincoln, to make an attack upon Richmond. Now, between Washington and Richmond the country was most difficult—wooded, marshy, cut by rivers—and McClellan believed that the best way in which to attack Richmond was not by the direct approach, but by a roundabout route. He decided to ship his troops by sea to the Peninsula between the York and James rivers and then to march upon Richmond up the peninsula across country which offered less natural obstruction. The drawback of this plan was that it would leave no army between Washington and Richmond to protect the Union capital. McClellan argued that if he made a vigorous attack in strength upon Richmond, the manœuvre would draw off the Confederate forces, and that the capture of Richmond would finally remove all threat to Washington. Lincoln, however, was persuaded to provide for the defence of Washington, and he ordered the organisation of three armies for the purpose—one in Western Virginia under Frémont, the explorer and Republican candidate of 1856, one in the Shenandoah valley under Banks, to guard the back door to Washington, and a third under McDowell in Washington itself. So McClellan set off, deprived of some of those troops upon which he had counted. Nor did he have any chance of getting them, for the Confederate general Stonewall Jackson tied up the three defending armies by a series of clever manœuvres until the end of June. He then moved his own forces to Richmond and joined General Robert E. Lee in the defence against McClellan. On June 25, 1862, began the seven days' battle before Richmond in which McClellan's army was repulsed. He held on throughout July and the army was recalled to Washington in August.

Meanwhile Lincoln had replaced McClellan as General-in-Chief by Henry W. Halleck, and had placed General Pope in charge of the three armies defending Washington—those of Frémont, Banks and McDowell. But Pope was no more successful. Towards the end of August he was defeated at the second battle of Bull Run, and on September 2 McClellan was called upon to resume command. General Lee moved his forces up the Shenandoah valley into Maryland in the hope of causing that state to rise and join the Southern side, and so to isolate and capture Washington. McClellan slowly followed him and missed his chance of attacking Lee's forces when they were divided. At last, on September 17, the armies met along the banks of Antietam Creek, a tributary of the Potomac, near Sharpsburg, in Maryland. McClellan's superior forces defeated Lee, though with great losses. But once more he failed to exploit his victory, and in spite of all the hints and orders of Lincoln, McClellan did not follow until five weeks had elapsed. In November Lincoln relieved him of his command and appointed General Burnside in his place. But Burnside did no better. He fought the Confederate troops at Fredericksburg in Virginia, but was defeated.

So in the eastern theatre the year 1862 had seen no deci-

sive move by either side. The war was seen to be costly and
bitter. A new element came into the struggle after the battle
of Antietam. Lincoln chose the relative victory of the Union
as the occasion for publishing his proclamation of emancipation for slaves in certain areas. He declared that on January
1, 1863, "all persons held as slaves within any state or desig-
nated part of a state the people whereof shall be in rebellion
against the United States shall be then, thenceforward and
forever free." This proclamation, made public on September
22, had as its object the strengthening of the Northern cause
from the military point of view. It was made by Lincoln as
Commander-in-Chief, and it related only to those parts of the
United States actually in rebellion. A fuller discussion of its
meaning and its place in the history of the Civil War is undertaken in Chapter 11.

The western theatre of the war in 1862 presented a contrast to the eastern. Here a steady advance in the fortunes of
the Union can be traced. The strategic importance of this
area for the Union's attack on the South lies in the fact that
it contained a system of water and rail communications by
which the Northern forces could penetrate right into the
Southern states at a variety of points and in the end come
down to the lowest part of the South and so advance up to
Virginia, encircling the whole area. There was the Mississippi,
the Ohio joining it, and two tributaries of the Ohio, the
Cumberland and the Tennessee, the last two running into
Kentucky, Tennessee and Alabama. There were railways in-
tersecting these rivers at points, the command of which was of
great importance to the opposing sides. The fighting was a
combination of naval and military warfare, with gun-boats
on the rivers acting in co-operation with land forces, and with
naval forces operating from the Gulf of Mexico working up
the Mississippi to effect a junction with those of the North.
The whole scheme was not carried through in 1862, but a
substantial part of it was accomplished.

The Union's operations in this theatre are associated largely
with the name of Ulysses S. Grant, acting at this time under
the orders of General Halleck, before the latter had been
appointed to succeed McClellan as General-in-Chief. The
Confederates had established defensive fortifications at points

on the Mississippi, Tennessee and Cumberland rivers to prevent the Union forces from advancing along them into the states of Tennessee and Kentucky. There was Island No. 10 on the Mississippi, Fort Henry on the Tennessee and Fort Donelson on the Cumberland. Quite early in the year 1862 the Union forces had dealt with these strong-points. Forces under Grant captured Fort Henry on February 6 and Fort Donelson on February 16. These, the first victories of the Union in the war, led to the occupation of Nashville, the capital of Tennessee, situated upon a railway which ran from the North right down into Georgia and South Carolina. Island No. 10 was captured in April. At the same time the Union obtained its second great victory at the battle of Shiloh, where 100,000 men were engaged on both sides and 20,000 of them were casualties. The result of the battle was that Corinth, an important railway junction, and, later, Memphis, on the junction of the Mississippi with the railway, were evacuated by the South. In this way the Union came to control the Mississippi down to Vicksburg. About the same time a naval force under Farragut bombarded the Southern forts at the mouth of the Mississippi, and finally, weary of trying to reduce them, ran past them and captured New Orleans. In this way the Union gained a mastery over the lower Mississippi.

All this had been achieved by April 1862. Vicksburg alone remained on the Mississippi as a Confederate post of any importance. A second Confederate line had its strongest point at Chattanooga on the Tennessee river and the railway farther to the east of Corinth and Memphis. But nothing was done in 1862 to conquer what remained, though Grant was anxious to act. It was not until 1863 that the western theatre came finally under Union control. On July 4, 1863, Grant captured Vicksburg. When, five days later, a smaller fortification, Fort Hudson, far down the river in Louisiana, also surrendered, the Union had command of the whole stretch of the Mississippi and encircled the South. "The Father of Waters," said Lincoln in a memorable phrase, "again goes unvexed to the sea." By two further battles, Chickamauga, in Georgia, on September 19–20, and Chattanooga on November 23–25, the Confederate armies were overcome, though with tremendous losses on both sides. The Union thus stood, in the winter of 1863, in a position of great strategic possibilities.

In the eastern theatre, no such startling possibilities had been opened up in 1863. The same story seemed to be told again that had been told in 1861 and 1862. Generals are appointed; they lose battles and they are superseded. On December 13, 1862, General Burnside, superseding McClellan, had been defeated at Fredericksburg, Virginia, as already mentioned. He was superseded by General Hooker, who, on May 2–4, lost the battle of Chancellorsville, near Fredericksburg. In June Hooker was removed and General Meade was appointed in his stead. Meade obtained a victory. Lee had advanced into Pennsylvania. The armies fought at Gettysburg and Lee was obliged to withdraw. His casualties were 22,000. Meade's were 18,000. But Gettysburg, like Antietam in 1862, was not followed up with sufficient vigour. Lee retired into Virginia and resumed his position standing guard over Richmond.

The victory of Gettysburg was on July 3, 1863, that of Vicksburg on July 4. They were great gains for the Union. The crisis of the war was past; the future of the Union was never so dark again. In November Lincoln attended the dedication of a cemetery at Gettysburg, and made the short speech, the Gettysburg speech, or oration, as it is called, which became so famous later as a statement of the belief of the Union in freedom. But while Vicksburg was a victory which opened up great possibilities, Gettysburg started nothing. The defensive strategy of Lee had held the Confederate line through both battles of Bull Run, the Peninsula campaign, Antietam, Fredericksburg, Chancellorsville and even Gettysburg. Meade was no nearer to Richmond than McClellan had been.

And in 1864 Lee's magnificent powers of defence continued to be seen. Ulysses S. Grant was placed in control of all the armies of the Union on March 10. He created, with Sherman, a great plan for converging upon the Confederacy from the north, west and south, and steadily reducing it to powerlessness. But in the eastern theatre, where Grant himself was in command, he found the plan most difficult to execute. He fought three great engagements—at the Wilderness near

Chancellorsville on May 5–6; at Spottsylvania Court House, about ten miles south-east of the Wilderness, on May 10–12; and at Cold Harbour, less than fifteen miles north-east of Richmond, on May 31. But from none of them did he obtain victory. He had reduced the Confederate numbers, but the result so far was stalemate. Grant was obliged to try another plan. He withdrew his forces and began to make a new approach from the south upon Richmond, laying siege to Petersburg, twenty miles due south of Richmond, on the Appomattox river, in June 1864. For the rest of the year the siege continued. Lee managed to hold out, though his cause was weakening.

It was weakening, not because of Grant's siege, but because of the enormous success of that part of Grant's plan which was being carried out in the western theatre by Sherman. In 1864, while Grant was fighting in the Wilderness, Sherman set out from Chattanooga along the line of the Western and Atlantic Railroad, towards Atlanta in Georgia, about 110 miles away. On September 2 Atlanta fell. He announced at once that he proposed to destroy all factories and public stores, so that the city should not be available again for the Confederate army. It had become their greatest source of supplies. Atlanta was set on fire, after non-combatants had been withdrawn, and Sherman set out on his march across Georgia towards the sea. On December 21 he reached Savannah on the coast. This, with the capture of the port of Mobile, on the Gulf of Mexico, by Farragut in the previous August, placed all the important sea bases in Union hands. And these successes perhaps did as much as anything to secure the re-election of Lincoln to the Presidency, against General McClellan, in November 1864.

In 1865 the consequences of Sherman's march and the whole strategy of Grant in the western theatre became apparent. Sherman began to march north from Savannah on January 14; a little over a month later he captured Columbia, the capital of South Carolina, and on the same day, February 18th, Charleston surrendered to the Union fleet. Sherman continued his advance to the north. Lee realised that the fall of Petersburg and then of Richmond was now a matter of time. He began to withdraw his forces, and Grant's armies prepared to close upon him. On March 29 their forward movement began. On April 2 Petersburg was taken by storm. On April 3 President Davis and the Confederate government left Richmond. On April 4 Lincoln visited Richmond and walked through the capital, almost unattended. On April 9 Lee surrendered to Grant at Appomattox Court House in Virginia. That was the end of the fighting.

Chapter 8

The Head of the Union

> "While I live and breathe,
> I mean to save the Union if I can,
> And by whatever means my hands can find
> Under the Constitution."
> STEPHEN VINCENT BENÉT: *John Brown's Body*.

THE PRESIDENCY OF the United States is in modern times the greatest secular office to which a man may be elected by the free votes of his fellows. It has not always been so. Many forces have operated to make it what it is now. Not least among them was the tenure of the office by Abraham Lincoln himself. Lincoln stands with Thomas Jefferson, Andrew Jackson, Woodrow Wilson and Franklin D. Roosevelt as one of the men who, by their own holding of the office, made the Presidency a greater office than it had been before. This does not mean that their successors necessarily lived up to the potentialities of the office. In many cases they proved to be weak and unimpressive. But the office itself became greater through the work of these great Presidents and it gave greater opportunities to men even of ordinary intelligence and honest, energetic ability. It is of some interest, therefore, to consider in detail the story of Lincoln's Presidency.

Within the office of President of the United States there are comprised three distinct functions which in few countries are held by the same officer—the function of head of the Union, the function of head of the government and the function of Commander-in-Chief. In the United Kingdom, for example, the King is the head of the state, and the Commander-in-Chief of all his forces, but the Prime Minister is the head of the government. In many European republics there has been a President with powers similar to those of the British King—the head of the state and the nominal Commander-in-Chief, but he has not been the head of the government. In the United States the President has all three functions, and there is no reason why he should not exercise them all to the full. In studying Lincoln's Presidency, it will be best to consider each of his functions separately, and to begin with that of head of the Union.

In normal times the President's function as head of the Union is important and valuable; he is the symbol that the states are united. In Lincoln's time, as in no other, his function as head of the Union was in the very forefront of controversy and struggle. For with his election, the states of the lower South declared that they had left the Union, and when they attempted to put their decision into effect, war began. Then it became clear that for Lincoln his function as head of the Union was all-important, for he was prepared to maintain the Union by force of arms if necessary. There was nothing new in this. He had always held this view. In the course of the Presidential campaign of 1856, when he was speaking for Frémont, he had said at Galena, Illinois:

"We, the majority, would not strive to dissolve the Union; and if any attempt is made, it must be by you, who so loudly stigmatise us as disunionists. But the Union, in any event, will not be dissolved. We don't want to dissolve it, and if you attempt it, we won't let you. With the purse and sword, the army and navy and treasury, in our hands and at our command, you could not do it. This government would be very weak indeed, if a majority with a disciplined army and navy and a well-filled treasury could not preserve itself when attacked by an unarmed, undisciplined, unorganised majority. All this talk about the dissolution of the Union is humbug, nothing but folly. We do not want to dissolve the Union; you shall not."

Lincoln's devotion to the Union is, in its intensity and supremacy, almost startling. He was prepared to go much farther to prevent the break-up of the Union than ever he proposed to go to prevent the extension of slavery. Yet he is usually thought of primarily as the liberator of slaves and the great enemy of slavery. He had said himself that slavery was a wrong and that its extension in the Territories of the United States should be resisted. But he never said that it should be resisted by the secession of the North from the Union or by the expulsion of the South from the Union, and above all he never said that it should be resisted by force of arms. He was ready to see the slavery question settled by vote and to abide by the result, and this, too, although he felt sure that the result would be that the United States became all slave or all free. But none the less he held that whether the Union be a free Union or a slave Union, he was determined that he must preserve the Union. And when he came in the course of the war to proclaim the emancipation of slaves, he did so as a measure to help preserve the Union; it was a measure of military necessity. Abraham Lincoln went to war, not to prevent or abolish slavery, but to preserve the Union of which he had been elected head.

There is much in Lincoln's attitude here that is puzzling. His attitude to slavery is perhaps not so puzzling as his attitude to the Union. After all, as will have been appreciated from the account given so far, Lincoln's attitude on slavery was consistent all through his political life. He opposed its extension in the Territories, but he opposed also interference with slavery in the states; and whenever he considered abolition, it was gradual and with compensation. He was on the slavery issue a moderate, not an abolitionist and not an extensionist. Yet, if this were so, when the states of the lower South seceded, why not let them go? They were slave states; Lincoln did not advocate interfering with slavery in them; outside the Union they could have no influence upon Union policy, no influence upon the Territories. Surely it would have been better, from the point of view of preventing the extension of slavery, to let them go? That was what some people in the North advocated. In January 1861, before Lincoln's inauguration, Horace Greeley used the phrase: "Wayward sisters, depart in peace." And, who knows, had they gone, might they not, after a decade or so, have abolished slavery, and have been ready to return to the Union? To none of these arguments was Lincoln prepared to assent. The Union must be preserved. There could be no half-measures here.

It would not be accurate to say that whereas on the slavery question Lincoln was a moderate, on the Union question he was an extremist. In one respect he was an extremist on both questions: he desired without qualification that all men everywhere should be free, and he desired without qualification that the Union should be preserved. But whereas on the slavery question he was content to defer to the wishes of the minority, on the Union question he was not. As he said himself, in regard to his plan for the abolition of slavery on December 1, 1861, "This would be compromise; but it would be compromise among the friends, and not with the enemies of the Union." Yet even on the Union question his methods, though firm from the first, were not extreme. He did not immediately make war upon the seceding states. His messages and speeches had a note of conciliation in them. In February 1861, on his journey to Washington for his inauguration, he said to the state assembly of New Jersey: "I shall do all that may be in my power to promote a peaceful settlement of all our difficulties. The man does not live who is more devoted to peace than I am, none who would do more to preserve it, but it may be necessary to put the foot down firmly." Always there was this note of conciliation, but with it the determination to maintain the Union. On the issues that divided North and South, and especially upon the issue of slavery, Lincoln was prepared to negotiate, to be moderate, to compromise, but it must be negotiation inside the Union. On the question of the Union there could be no negotiation, no compromise.

In his First Inaugural Address on March 4, 1861, the position was clearly stated: "In your hands, my dissatisfied fellow-countrymen," he said, addressing the South, "and not in mine is the momentous issue of civil war. The government will not assail you. You can have no conflict without being yourselves the aggressors." But to this was added this significant sentence: "You have no oath registered in Heaven to destroy the government, while I shall have the most solemn one to 'preserve, protect and defend' it." When, at Fort Sumter, the Union's forces were attacked, the act of aggression had been committed, and Lincoln was ready at once to resist with force.

How did Lincoln justify his supreme devotion to the Union? First of all, he believed that secession was illegal; it was contrary to the terms of the Constitution of the United

States. In his First Inaugural he said: "I hold, that in contemplation of universal law and of the Constitution, the Union of these states is perpetual." The legality of secession was a subject of intense dispute in the days of the Civil War and afterwards. It was not only the South which believed in the legality of secession. There were men both in North and South who were Unionists at the time of Lincoln's election, but who none the less believed in the legality of secession, although they did not favour its exercise in this particular case. The most careful exposition of the legality of secession was found indeed in the writings of Alexander H. Stephens, who, as was mentioned earlier, favoured the maintenance of the Union and advised his own state, Georgia, not to secede. When secession was decided upon, he went with his state and became Vice-President of the Confederacy.[1]

Was Lincoln's view of the Constitution correct? If the Constitution itself is considered as an isolated document, there is no doubt that it contains no provision, express or implied, conferring a unilateral right of secession upon any state, whether upon the government of the state or the people of the state. It was true that the Tenth Amendment to the Constitution, passed in 1791, gave some support to the contention of the secessionists. It ran: "The powers not delegated to the United States by the Constitution, nor prohibited by it to the states, are reserved to the states respectively, or to the people." It now became a matter of argument what powers had been delegated to the United States. The argument of the secessionists was that, whatever powers had been delegated, the states—and by the states they meant the people of the states, not the governments—had retained their sovereignty and were thus fully empowered, if they thought fit, to withdraw from the Union. The Tenth Amendment, in the opinion of Jefferson Davis, for example, as stated in his First Message to the Confederate Congress, had placed "beyond any pretence of doubt the reservation by the states of all their sovereign rights and powers not expressly delegated to the United States by the Constitution."

[1] His case is stated in *A Constitutional View of the Late War Between the States*.

So there arose the question whether or not "sovereignty" had actually been surrendered by the states. The discussion of this question soon involved an historical argument. What had the framers of the Constitution themselves believed that they had done? Did they think that they had created a sovereign government over the states, or did they believe that they had left sovereignty entirely with the states? On this broader historical argument it is necessary to say that there was a good case on both sides. The Fathers of the Constitution had not all thought the same thing and some of them had not spoken unambiguously. Lincoln had a case; so had Jefferson Davis and Stephens. And of the two, it must be said that Lincoln overstated his case. He said in his First Inaugural: "The Union is much older than the Constitution. It was formed, in fact, by the Articles of Association in 1774. It was matured and continued by the Declaration of Independence in 1776. It was further matured and the faith of all the then thirteen states expressly plighted and engaged that it should be perpetual, by the Articles of Confederation in 1778. And finally, in 1787, one of the declared objects for ordaining and establishing the Constitution was 'to form a more perfect Union.'" In fact, although some form of association between the states was older than the Constitution, those forms of association were different from the Union. The Union which existed in 1861 was produced by the Constitution. To say that it was older was to fall back on an historical error.

Taking Lincoln's case moderately, however, and putting it beside the secessionist case, it is not easy to say by a reference to the opinions of the Fathers of the Constitution which was the true interpretation. But the contest in 1861 was carried on in extreme terms. The secessionists claimed full sovereignty for the states; their opponents claimed full sovereignty for the Union. What the Constitution of the United States actually did was to divide sovereignty between the Union and the states. It created a government for the Union, not a mere agent of the states; it left governments for the states, not mere subordinate administrative agencies. But the contestants of 1861 could not speak in terms of divided sovereignty. The political conceptions of an absolutist theory of sovereignty were still accepted. It was only after the Civil War, when the doctrine of the right of secession was defeated by force of arms, that its historical and logical foundations became discredited. The South had a case which was strong in past history, but it proved to have no future.

Some passages from Lincoln's message to the special session of Congress which he called for July 4, 1861, show his argument at its best:

"Unquestionably the States have the powers and rights reserved to them in and by the national Constitution; but among these, surely, are not included all conceivable powers, however mischievous or destructive; but, at most, such only as were known in the world at the time, as governmental powers; and, certainly, a power to destroy the government itself had never been known as a governmental—as a merely administrative power. This relative matter of national power and State rights, as a principle, is no other than the principle of generality and locality. Whatever concerns the whole should be confided to the whole—to the General Government; while whatever concerns only the State should be left exclusively to the State. This is all there is of original principle about it. . . ."

One result of the victory of the North in the Civil War was that the view of the Union as indestructible came to prevail. It received official sanction from the Supreme Court in 1868 in the case of *Texas v. White*. The language used by the Court in this case follows so closely the line of reasoning set forth by Lincoln in his First Inaugural and in his First Message to Congress, that it is worth while quoting a passage. For in this way some notion may be gained of the influence which Lincoln had upon the idea of American Union:

"It is needless to discuss at length the question whether the right of a State to withdraw from the Union for any cause, regarded by herself as sufficient, is consistent with the Constitution of the United States. The union of the States never was a purely artificial and arbitrary relation. It began among the colonies, and grew out of common origin, mutual sympathies, kindred principles, similar interests, and geographical relations. It was confirmed and strengthened by the necessities of war, and received definite form, and character, and sanction from the Articles of Confederation. By these the Union was solemnly declared to 'be perpetual.' And when these Articles were found to be inadequate to the exigencies of the country, the Constitution was ordained 'to form a more perfect union.' It is difficult to convey the idea of indissoluble unity more clearly than by these words. What can be indissoluble if a perpetual union, made more perfect, is not? But the perpetuity and indissolubility of the Union by no means implies the loss of distinct and individual existence, or of the right of self-government by the States. Under the Articles of Confederation each State retained its sovereignty, freedom and independence, and every power, jurisdiction and right not expressly delegated to the United States. Under the Constitution, though the powers of the States were much restricted, still, all powers not delegated to the United States, nor prohibited to the States, are reserved to the States respectively, or to the people. And we have said . . . 'the people of each State compose a State, having its own government, and endowed with all the functions essential to separate and independent existence,' and that 'without the states in union, there could be no such political body as the United States.' Not only therefore can there be no loss of separate and independent autonomy to the states, through their union under the Constitution, but it may be not unreasonably said that the preservation of the states, and the maintenance of their governments, are as much within the design and care of the Constitution as the preservation of the Union and the maintenance of the National government. The Constitution in all its provisions looks to an indestructible Union, composed of indestructible states."

From this argument the Supreme Court concluded that Texas, notwithstanding its ordinance of secession, "continued to be a state and a state of the Union." This had been Lincoln's view throughout the war. He considered, as he said in his First Inaugural, "that in view of the Constitution and the laws, the Union is unbroken," and he acted upon this belief, not merely in the work of suppressing rebellion, but, as will be seen later, in planning the reconstruction of the divided Union.

But the dispute between Lincoln and the seceders was not merely a legal dispute. Both sides were anxious, it is true, to prove that their actions were legal. But they believed also that they were morally justified in the action they took, and they were supported throughout in their conflict by the sense of moral rightness. Here one leaves the ground of a legal right of secession and moves to the ground of a moral right of rebellion or revolution. Abraham Lincoln could not deny, in the light of his country's history, that there were circumstances in which, in the words of the American Declaration of Independence in 1776, "it becomes necessary for one people to dissolve the political bonds which have connected them with another." He admitted the existence of the moral right to rebel. But he asserted that in 1860 and 1861 the seceding states had no adequate justification for exercising this right. And he gave several reasons for so thinking.

First of all, he said that secession did not provide the remedy for the grievances which the South professed to have. For what was the dispute? "One section of our country believes slavery is right, and ought to be extended, while the other believes it is wrong, and ought not to be extended." How can secession solve this problem? It makes the extension of slavery impossible, so that the South gains nothing there. It makes it harder, not easier, to deal with questions like fugitive slaves and tariffs. Yet these questions are bound to arise, for the two unions will be side by side. "The foreign slave trade, now imperfectly suppressed, would be ultimately revived, without restriction, in one section, while fugitive slaves, now only partially surrendered, would not be surrendered at all by the other. . . . Suppose you go to war, you cannot fight always; and when, after much loss on both sides, and no gain on either, you cease fighting, the identical old questions as to terms of intercourse are again upon you." These words were used in his First Inaugural. The argument was developed in more detail in his Annual Message to Congress in December 1862. Secession is ineffectual as a means of settling the disputes. It will achieve nothing except to break up the Union. It achieves a wrong and it sets nothing right.

And this leads Lincoln to his next argument. He believes

not only that secession in morally unjustified because it will do no good; he believes also that it will do positive harm. It will be a blow to democratic and free government all over the world. It will make people believe that democratic government lacks the qualities necessary for good and effective government. In his First Message to Congress, in their special session, July 4, 1861, he used these words:

"This issue embraces more than the fate of these United States. It presents to the whole family of man the question whether a constitutional republic or democracy—a government of the people by the same people—can or cannot maintain its territorial integrity against its own domestic foes. It presents the question whether discontented individuals, too few in numbers to control administration according to organic law in any case, can always, upon the pretences made in this case or any other pretences, or arbitrarily without any pretence, break up their government and thus practically put an end to free government upon the earth. It forces us to ask: 'Is there, in all republics, this inherent and fatal weakness?' 'Must a government, of necessity, be too strong for the liberties of its own people, or too weak to maintain its own existence?' "

And it was this same idea he had in mind when he said, in the famous remarks at Gettysburg on November 19, 1863, that the Civil War was testing whether a nation "conceived in liberty and dedicated to the proposition that all men are created equal" could long endure; that the object of the war was to ensure "that government of the people, by the people, and for the people, shall not perish from the earth." Lincoln opposed secession because it struck a blow at democratic government.

Yet it is natural to ask, has a minority no right of rebellion in a democratic government? More particularly, if by democratic government is meant the rule of the majority, may there not be occasions when the majority is tyrannical or where the division of opinion between majority and minority is so acute, that the minority is entitled to leave? It is not certain what Lincoln's answer would be to a very general question of this sort. It is likely that he would admit that there could be circumstances in which a minority would be justified in rebelling against a majority. But in a true democracy, as he conceived it, where all sides had the right freely to advocate their view, the minority must acquiesce in the proposition of majority rule. More particularly was the South obliged to acquiesce when its right to perpetuate slavery in its own borders was conceded by the majority. Lincoln's argument seems to be that, although the majority may not always be right, the consequences of rejecting majority rule are so serious—they produce anarchy—that it is better to follow the majority than to rebel.

In his First Inaugural he said: "Plainly, the central idea of secession is the essence of anarchy. A majority held in restraint by constitutional checks and limitations, and always changing easily with deliberate changes of popular opinions and sentiments, is the only true sovereign of a free people. Whoever rejects it does, of necessity, fly to anarchy or to despotism. Unanimity is impossible; the rule of a minority, as a permanent arrangement, is wholly inadmissible; so that, rejecting the majority principle, anarchy or despotism in some form is all that is left." It was therefore justifiable in a democracy, when its central principle was attacked, to put down by force those who resisted it. This was the substance of a passage in the message to Congress at its special session in 1861:

"Our popular government has often been called an experiment. Two points in it our people have already settled—the successful establishing and the successful administering of it. One still remains—its successful maintenance against a formidable internal attempt to overthrow it. It is now for them to demonstrate to the world that those who can fairly carry on election can also suppress a rebellion: that ballots are the rightful and peaceful successors of bullets; and that when ballots have fairly and constitutionally decided, there can be no successful appeal back to bullets; that there can be no successful appeal, except to ballots themselves, at succeeding elections. Such will be a great lesson of peace; teaching men that what they cannot take by an election, neither can they take by a war, teaching all the folly of being the beginners of a war."

This is a hard saying for a permanent minority. It means that they must acquiesce perpetually in a line of political

action of which they disapprove. Majority rule and the ballot
box hold out hope to a minority that has some likelihood of
becoming itself a majority one day. But for the South there
seemed no such likelihood. Be the government as democratic
as it possibly could be, with every safeguard of free speech,
the slave states were now in a minority and they could never
become a majority. Their way of life, their social organisation, could not prevail; on the contrary, they might well suffer
in the Union. What comfort was there for them in recourse
to the ballot box? What chance for them in a system of
majorities "always changing easily with deliberate changes of
popular opinions and sentiments?" That was the position of
the South. Yet it seems clear that Lincoln held fast to the
view that, permanent minority as they were, they must acquiesce in the views of the majority. To do otherwise would be
wrong, for it would destroy government.

It is startling to realise that Lincoln did not believe in the
principle of self-determination of peoples. The South claimed
themselves to be a distinct people; they strove for independence as the Irish strove to free themselves from the United
Kingdom. Yet Lincoln fought against them with more determination than any British Prime Minister fought against Ire-
land in the nineteenth and twentieth centuries. Perhaps Gladstone's sympathy for the South is more understandable if this
aspect of the case is considered. He saw them as a nation
struggling to be free. "Jefferson Davis and other leaders of
the South," he said, "have made an army; they are making,
it appears, a navy; and they have made—what is more than
either—they have made a nation." Gladstone's statement was
resented by the North and remembered against him. It was
certainly unwise, because he was a Cabinet Minister at the
time. But he made it because he favoured the rights of small
nations.

To those who associate the principle of self-determination
with the United States it comes as something of a shock to
find that Abraham Lincoln, associated in one's mind with
liberty and democracy, should argue so firmly against it. Yet
the fact is unavoidable. Woodrow Wilson, the greatest President of the United States between Lincoln and Franklin
Roosevelt, advocated the principle of self-determination for

the settlement of national-minority problems in Europe. He was not a blind and absolute believer in the efficiency of the principle, nor, we may assert, was Lincoln a blind and absolute opponent of it. But Woodrow Wilson may be said to have given pre-eminence to self-determination, to secession and to disintegration as agents for good government; Lincoln gave pre-eminence to majority rule, to union and integration. It is interesting to notice that Lincoln was a Republican and Wilson a Democrat; Lincoln was a Westerner, a frontiersman, allied with the North; Wilson was a Southerner, and, when Lincoln delivered his First Inaugural, he was a little boy of five, living in a Presbyterian parsonage in Augusta, Georgia, one of the seceding and Confederate states of America.

Yet ruthless as Lincoln's determination was to put down secession and to preserve the Union by force, he retained always a sublime gift of seeing all the states, whether seceded or wavering or united, as part of the Union. He never spoke in revengeful terms of the seceded states, and he never thought of them as outcasts or foreigners. One of the finest examples of this is his great oration at Gettysburg in 1863, where he spoke upon a battlefield where the dead of Union and of Confederate armies still lay unburied. There was no revenge in his speech and no talk of victory. It is so great an oration that it deserves reproduction here in full.

Lincoln was not the orator of the day. Those responsible for the dedicatory ceremonies had invited Edward Everett, a former Secretary of State, ex-president of Harvard University, a great scholar and man of letters, to deliver the oration of the day. Lincoln was invited to attend the ceremony a little more than a fortnight beforehand. When the day came Everett delivered a fine oration of two hours or so in length. Lincoln followed with a few words he had written out rather carefully. They were not received with any particular enthusiasm at the moment, but there is an obvious explanation of this. Lincoln's words were heard by only a few hundred people of the many thousands gathered at Gettysburg. For he had a poor speaking voice—rather squeaky and high-pitched—and the gathering was, of course, in the open air. After Everett's fine delivery, Lincoln's voice was not effective. And in any case the spectators were more interested in the efforts of a photographer to get a picture of the President speaking than in what he was actually saying.[2] But when the speech was published it soon became famous; in Lincoln's lifetime it was already in great demand. And since that time valiant research workers have examined every line and word of the speech to determine its meaning and authenticity. In particular the phrase "government of the people, by the people, for the people" has been traced to various sources, in an attempt to discover if, in Lincoln's oration, it was original. It seems likely that Lincoln had already seen it, perhaps in the writings of Theodore Parker, an abolitionist preacher, who in 1850 spoke of "democracy, that is, a government of all the people, by all the people, for all the people." But it matters not who said it before Lincoln. If Lincoln had not said it, it would not now be said.

As head of the Union, President Lincoln spoke these words at Gettysburg on November 19, 1863:

"Four score and seven years ago our fathers brought forth on this continent a new nation, conceived in liberty, and dedicated to the proposition that all men are created equal.

"Now we are engaged in a great civil war, testing whether that nation, or any nation so conceived and so dedicated, can long endure. We are met on a great battlefield of that war. We have come to dedicate a portion of that field as a final resting place for those who here gave their lives that that nation might live. It is altogether fitting and proper that we should do this.

"But, in a larger sense, we cannot dedicate—we cannot consecrate—we cannot hallow—this ground. The brave men, living and dead, who struggled here, have consecrated it far above our poor power to add or detract. The world will little note, nor long remember, what we say here, but it can never forget what they did here. It is for us the living, rather, to be

[2] The photographer failed. This was in the days before newspaper photographers had developed to its full efficiency their shameless and ruthless technique which permits them nowadays to stand in the forefront of any national occasion, however solemn, and obliterate for the spectators all sight and sound of the ceremonies by the operation of their cameras.

dedicated here to the unfinished work which they who fought here have thus far so nobly advanced. It is rather for us to be here dedicated to the great task remaining before us—that from these honored dead we take increased devotion to that cause for which they gave the last full measure of devotion—that we here highly resolve that these dead shall not have died in vain—that this nation, under God,[3] shall have a new birth of freedom—and that government of the people, by the people, for the people, shall not perish from the earth."

[3] These words, "under God," were not in the written draft Lincoln held in his hand; he added them while speaking.

Chapter 9

The Commander-in-Chief

"If I could move that battle with my hands!
No, it don't work. I'm not a general.
All I can do is trust the men who are."
STEPHEN VINCENT BENÉT: *John Brown's Body.*

THE PRESIDENT OF the United States is not only the head of
the Union, he is, in the words of the Constitution,
"Commander-in-Chief of the army and the navy of the
United States, and of the militia of the several states, when
called into the actual service of the United States." These two
functions of head of the state and Commander-in-Chief are
commonly united in the person of the same officer in the constitutions of modern states, but when this is done it is not
always intended that the exercise of the powers of
Commander-in-Chief should be more than nominal. In the
United States, however, where the President was intended to
be more than a figurehead, it was not to be assumed that he
would not exercise his powers in all his capacities. In the
case of Abraham Lincoln it is found that his use of his
powers as Commander-in-Chief brought in a new conception
of the President's rôle in this office, and left a permanent
mark upon the governmental system of the United States.

There are two aspects in which Lincoln's exercise of his
powers may be studied. In the first place, it is worth while to
study his interpretation of the scope of these powers—what,
in his view, were the powers which the President was entitled
to exercise in his capacity as Commander-in-Chief. This will
involve a consideration of what he considered the proper
functions of Congress in the sphere of war powers. The second aspect of the question is the actual exercise of such
powers as, in Lincoln's view, pertained to the Commander-in-
Chief. What were his relations as a layman with the professional soldiers? By what method did he execute the powers

which in law were confided to him? Each of these two aspects will be treated in turn.

Let us begin with the scope of the powers of the President as Commander-in-Chief. It is worth noting that the Constitution of the United States does not by any means confer the whole of what is loosely called "the war power" upon the President. For one thing the power to declare war is not given to him; it is given to Congress—that is to both Houses, the House of Representatives and the Senate. Further, Congress, not the President, is given power "to raise and support armies," "to provide and maintain a navy," "to make rules for the government and regulation of the land and naval forces," "to provide for calling forth the militia to execute the laws of the Union, suppress insurrections and repel invasions," "to provide for organising, arming and disciplining the militia, and for governing such part of them as may be employed in the service of the United States."

From a study of these passages in the Constitution it would be reasonable to conclude that "the war power" of the President amounted to no more than the command of such armies and fleets as Congress provided. Lincoln himself had held this view strongly, it will be recalled, when, as a Congressman in 1848, he criticised President Polk's actions which had brought on the Mexican War. When his friend Herndon had criticised his view, he replied in this passage:

"Allow the President to invade a neighbouring nation whenever he shall deem it necessary to repel an invasion and you allow him to do so whenever he may choose to say he deems it necessary for such purpose—and you allow him to make war at pleasure. Study to see if you can fix any limit in this respect, after you have given him so much as you propose. . . . The provision of the Constitution giving the war-making power to Congress was dictated, as I understand it, by the following reasons: Kings had always been involving and impoverishing their people in wars, pretending generally, if not always, that the good of the people was their object. This, our convention understood to be the most oppressive of all kingly oppressions, and they resolved to so frame the Constitution that no one man should hold the power of bringing this oppression upon us. But your view destroys the whole matter, and places our President where kings have always stood."

There was a good deal to be said for this view. It was advocated by many members of both Houses of Congress during the Civil War. But it was not the view which Lincoln himself adopted when he came to exercise his powers. When Fort Sumter was bombarded on April 14, 1861, Congress was not in session. When Lincoln resolved that force must be repelled by force, it might have been anticipated that he would have taken steps to call Congress together at the earliest moment, Congress, the body with power to raise armies and to provide for the calling forth of the militia to execute the laws of the Union and to suppress insurrections. In fact, he acted himself with promptness. Under the Militia Act of 1795 he was entitled to call forth the militia under certain conditions. Under the authority of this act, he issued his proclamation of April 15, stating that whereas the laws of the United States were opposed by combinations too powerful to be suppressed by the ordinary course of judicial proceedings, the militia of the several states of the Union, to the aggregate number of 75,000, was called forth to suppress the said combinations and cause the laws to be duly executed. The period of service under this call was to be three months. The Militia Act required also that Congress should be called together in such circumstances as these. Lincoln accordingly summoned Congress into special session, but he fixed its date of meeting as July 4—almost three month ahead.

Long before this date events had made it necessary for the President to take action upon a scale beyond that contemplated by the Militia Act. He proceeded without hesitation to perform acts which Congress was competent to perform and which, in the opinion of many, Congress alone was competent to perform. On May 3 a new proclamation was issued by which the President proposed to raise an Army. He called for 42,000 volunteers to serve for three years; he increased the regular Army of the United States by 23,000 men, and he added 18,000 men to the Navy for the blockade service. For none of these actions, all within the competence of Congress, had he any authorisation by Congressional Act. Money was needed to support these military preparations.

Lincoln gave orders for the purchase of ships and supplies which pledged the credit of the United States up to the sum of about a quarter of a billion dollars. He advanced $2,000,000 to a Union Safety Committee in New York from unappropriated funds in the Treasury of the United States. The Constitution said: "No money shall be drawn from the Treasury, but in consequence of appropriations made by law." To these actions was added a proclamation declaring a blockade of Southern ports; the writ of *habeas corpus* was suspended in certain places; orders were given for the arrest and detention of persons who were represented to the President as being engaged in or contemplating treasonable practices; and the post office was closed to treasonable correspondence. All this was done "either without one whit of statutory authority or with the merest figment thereof."

But was it unconstitutional? Lincoln thought not. He justified his actions to Congress when it met on July 4 by two lines of argument. First of all, he said that he had done nothing "beyond the constitutional competency of Congress," nothing, therefore, which Congress could not legalise by subsequent action. In this case Congress did legalise his acts. But the claim was interesting. It suggested that in an emergency the President could take action upon matters within the competence of Congress, trusting to Congressional approval at a later stage. This involved an extension of the Commander-in-Chief's powers beyond the narrower interpretation of them which Lincoln himself had favoured in his letter to Herndon. But he went farther than this. He claimed that in an emergency of this kind the President was endowed, under the Constitution, with powers in his own right, to take action to suppress rebellion and to safeguard the safety of the Union. These powers existed independently of Congressional powers, although in many matters they could be exercised concurrently. A good example of this view is his defence of his exercise of the power to suspend the writ of *habeas corpus*.

The Constitution of the United States says: "The privilege of the writ of *habeas corpus* shall not be suspended, unless when in cases of rebellion or invasion the public safety may require it." The Constitution does not say that Congress alone or the President alone or both may suspend the writ.

It is silent on this point. Lincoln believed that the President was entitled to suspend the writ independently of Congressional action, though he did not deny that Congress also might do so. His exercise of the power led him into conflict with Chief Justice Taney of the Supreme Court, who, in a famous case called *ex parte* Merryman, attempted to serve the writ upon a general who held as prisoner Merryman, an officer of a secessionist drill company in Maryland. The general refused to obey the writ, and Chief Justice Taney was obliged to put on record his opinion that the President's action in suspending the writ was unconstitutional.

Lincoln's problem was how to deal with activities which in modern times have come to be called "fifth column" and "quisling." There were those who discouraged enlistment, aided desertion, attempted sabotage on behalf of the South, destroyed enrolment lists, undertook espionage. The ordinary processes of Congressional legislation were not considered sufficient: neither the Conspiracies Act of July 31, 1861, nor the Treason Act of July 17, 1862, proved effective for controlling the anti-Union activities in the North. But before Congress had assembled on July 4, 1861, Lincoln had issued his proclamation of April 27 suspending the writ of *habeas corpus*, and he continued to issue such proclamations after Congressional action had been taken. On September 24, 1862, a general proclamation was issued providing that "during the existing insurrections and as a necessary measure for suppressing the same, all rebels and insurgents, their aiders and abettors within the United States, and all persons discouraging volunteer enlistments, resisting militia drafts, or guilty of any disloyal practice affording aid and comfort to rebels against the authority of the United States, shall be subject to martial law, and liable to trial and punishment by court martial or military commissions," and persons so arrested and punished were denied the privilege of the writ of *habeas corpus*. The number of persons arrested under these provisions ran into thousands. Over 13,000 cases were listed in the records of the Federal commissary-general of prisons, and to this must be added those arrested by the Navy and the State Department.

Lincoln justified this action repeatedly. A famous passage

in the message to Congress at its special session on July 4, 1861, may be quoted, but similar statements can be found in two letters—one to Erastus Corning, dated June 12, 1863, and the other to M. Birchard, dated June 29, 1863, both of which are printed in Volume 2 of Lincoln's *Works*. He claimed first that the Constitution gave him power to suspend the writ in the express terms set out. But over and above all this he claimed the duty to save the Constitution by breaking one small part of it, if that proved necessary. The two points are set out as follows:

"The provision of the Constitution 'that the privilege of the writ of *habeas corpus* shall not be suspended, unless when, in cases of rebellion or invasion, the public safety may require it,' is equivalent to a provision—is a provision—that such privilege may be suspended when, in case of a rebellion or an invasion, the public safety does require it. It was decided that we have a case of rebellion, and that the public safety does require the qualified suspension of the privilege of the writ which was authorised to be made. Now it is insisted that Congress, and not the Executive, is vested with this power. But the Constitution itself is silent as to which or who is to exercise the power; and as the provision was plainly made for a dangerous emergency, it cannot be believed the framers of the instrument intended that in every case the danger should run its course until Congress could be called together, the very assembling of which might be prevented, as was intended in this case, by the rebellion."

The second argument, the argument of overriding necessity to preserve the government, was made in the following passage:

"The whole of the laws which were required to be faithfully executed were being resisted and failing of execution in nearly one-third of the states. Must they be allowed to finally fail of execution, even had it been perfectly clear that by the use of the means necessary to their execution some single law, made in such extreme tenderness of the citizen's liberty that, practically, it relieves more of the guilty than of the innocent, should to a very limited extent be violated? To state the question more directly, are all the laws but one to go unexecuted, and the government itself go to pieces lest that one be violated? Even in such a case would not the official oath ['to take care that the laws be faithfully executed'] be broken if the government should be overthrown, when it was believed that disregarding the single law would tend to preserve it?"

The controversy between those who held that the President had the right to suspend the writ of *habeas corpus* and those who denied it was not settled even when Congress passed a *habeas corpus* act of March 3, 1863. In this act it was provided that "during the present rebellion, the President of the United States, whenever, in his judgement, the public safety may require it, is authorised to suspend the privilege of the writ of *habeas corpus* in any case throughout the United States, or any part thereof." But some maintained that in this act Congress was doing no more than recognising the right of the President to suspend the writ; others believed that Congress was actually conferring the right upon him. The ambiguous wording was intentional; it was a compromise to meet the conflicting views of those who favoured and those who opposed the principle of the exclusive power of Congress to suspend. The question remained open throughout the Civil War and afterwards; the Supreme Court as a whole—for Chief Justice Taney rendered his opinion alone, in a case tried on circuit—has not pronounced upon the point.

But Lincoln did not confine his claim to the possession of powers which Congress also might have. He asserted that as Commander-in-Chief the President could do things which Congress could not do. The great example of this assertion is his action to emancipate the slaves. Lincoln believed that Congress, even in war-time, had no power to interfere with slavery in the states. That was his opinion before he became President, as was seen in earlier chapters, and the progress of the war did not change his view. He did, in fact, assent to certain emancipating measures of Congress, although in July 1864, when Congress passed what was called the Wade-Davis Reconstruction Bill, which contained, among other things, a provision to emancipate the slaves in the rebel states, Lincoln refused to assent to it and in a proclamation stated his views in these words: "I am . . . unprepared . . . to declare a constitutional competency in Congress to abolish slavery in the states." Yet he claimed and exercised himself as Commander-in-Chief a power to emancipate slaves in certain areas.

The story of emancipation is told in a later chapter.[1] What must be stressed here is Lincoln's firm adherence to the view that only military necessity could justify his action. He issued his proclamation of September 22, 1862, "by virtue of the power in me vested as Commander-in-Chief of the army and navy . . . and as a fit and necessary war measure." It was an act "warranted by the Constitution upon military necessity." "As Commander-in-Chief," he once said, "I suppose I have a right to take any measure which may best subdue the enemy." "I think the Constitution invests the Commander-in-Chief with the law of war in time of war," and he believed that the law of war gave the right to take property "where taking it helps us or hurts the enemy." Speaking of the proclamation, he said it "has no constitutional or legal justification, except as a military measure." And this doctrine is borne out by the terms in which the proclamation was made. It applied only to states or parts of states actually under rebel control; those portions of Confederate territory which were under Union control were, in general, exempted from the terms of the proclamation. Nor, of course, was any emancipation decreed among slave states still loyal to the Union.

There is some doubt among constitutional authorities about the legality of Lincoln's action. He himself was not certain of it. And he saw also the difficulties that would arise if no more comprehensive action were taken. What, for example, would be the status of freed slaves after the war? Would those freed on grounds of military necessity remain free when the necessity was over? And what should be done for slaves in loyal states? These problems led Lincoln to advocate action by constitutional amendment, the course of which will be described later.

For this assumption of the war power to the extent so far described Lincoln was called a dictator in his own day, and it is still common to speak of his period of office as one of "Presidential dictatorship." Yet this term cannot be applied

[1] See Chapter 11.

accurately, if it is to be used in the sense and with the associations which it has in modern times. Professor James G. Randall made a careful and detailed study of the working of the United States Constitution in the Civil War period, the results of which were set out in his *Constitutional Problems Under Lincoln*. In his later book, *The Civil War and Reconstruction*, the best book on the subject so far written, he makes the following statement, based upon his earlier researches: "Lincoln's practice fell short of dictatorship as the word is understood in the fourth decade of the twentieth century. He did not think of suppressing his legislature and ruling without it. He did not pack his Congress or eject the opposition. There was nothing in his administration comparable to a Napoleonic *coup d'état* or a Cromwellian purging of Parliament. No party emblem was adopted as the flag of the country. No rule for the universal saluting of Lincoln was imposed. There was no Lincoln party constituting a super-state and visiting vengeance upon political opponents. Criminal violence was not employed *sub rosa* after the fashion of modern dictatorships. No undue advantage was taken of the emergency to force arbitrary rule upon the country to promote personal ends. Lincoln half expected to be defeated in 1864. The people were free to defeat him if they chose at the polls. The Constitution was indeed stretched, but it was not subverted."

Something may be said now of the other aspect of Lincoln's exercise of his powers as Commander-in-Chief. It concerns the problem of the proper relations between a civilian Commander-in-Chief and the military and naval men who are his expert advisers and the instruments through which his policies are to be executed. How far should the civilian interfere with military matters? The problem has arisen in the United States, not only in Lincoln's time, but later also, under the presidencies of Woodrow Wilson and Franklin D. Roosevelt. It has arisen in Britain under Lloyd George and Winston Churchill. No simple answer can be given to what is an extremely difficult question.

Yet, at the risk of appearing a little naïve and doctrinaire, one may suggest a few principles of an elementary kind which may be applicable to such a situation. If they do no more than serve as a useful method of judging Lincoln's record as Commander-in-Chief, they will have served their purpose. When Walter Bagehot considered the relations of a constitutional monarch in Britain with his Ministers, he suggested that the monarch had three rights—the right to be consulted, the right to encourage and the right to warn. And, he added, "a king of great sense and sagacity would want no others." Would it be reasonable to suggest that a civilian Commander-in-Chief possesses these same three rights in relation to his generals—the right to be consulted, the right to encourage and the right to warn? And if we add to these three two others, of undoubted validity—the right to appoint good generals and the right to dismiss bad ones—could we not say that, with these five, a President "of great sense and sagacity would want no others"? There is much in Lincoln's career as Commander-in-Chief which would seem to support this view. Let us review briefly what he did.

It may be said at once that Lincoln was not prepared to be a cipher. Though he might not intend to follow the advice of his Attorney-General, Edward Bates, who urged him to become "the Chief Commander" and "command the commanders," to exercise his full legal powers in fact, he did intend to exercise influence. Yet his equipment was so scanty —he knew nothing of strategy nor of military men. He was the essence of a civilian. Here he was at a disadvantage in comparison with President Jefferson Davis, who had himself acted as Secretary of War under President Polk, during the Mexican War, as was mentioned earlier, and who had an intimate knowledge of the officers and equipment of the United States Army. As many of these officers, in regular service, seceded with the Southern states, Jefferson Davis had to hand more than enough material from which to organise his high command. Lincoln had none of this knowledge and none of this material. He had to seek his best men by the costly process of trial and error.

Some indication of his experiments will have been gained from the short sketch of the course of the war given in a previous chapter. Lincoln was always subjected to political pressure and personal intrigue where the conduct of the war was concerned. Two factors in particular operated here.

There was the position of Washington, vulnerable to Confederate attack, which meant that the President was urged constantly to allow no military movement which would leave Washington undefended. The second factor was the existence of a Congressional Committee on the conduct of the war, which busied itself in inquiries and advice to the President. Lincoln was not always able to resist it.

When the war began Lincoln inherited Major-General Winfield Scott as his Chief of Staff—an old veteran of the Mexican and the Texan wars, whose methods were thorough and slow. Lincoln appointed McDowell to the command of the army in front of Washington, but the defeat of Bull Run meant that a change must be made. Scott made some complaint that Lincoln had forced him to act before he was ready. Lincoln denied the accusation and brought McClellan to Washington, first to succeed McDowell and soon to succeed Scott as General-in-Chief of the armies of the Union. It is in his relations with McClellan that Lincoln's participation in military affairs is most marked and his influence discussed with most controversy.

McClellan was only thirty-five when Lincoln appointed him to command the army of the Potomac. He was most efficient, thorough, a good disciplinarian, yet popular. Lincoln began by giving him his full confidence. McClellan set to work to organise an army which with one shattering blow would decide the war. He said himself that his plan was "to display such an overwhelming strength as will convince all our antagonists, especially those of the governing, aristocratic class, of the utter impossibility of resistance." But to do this, as McClellan wanted to do it, took a very long time. He was appointed in July 1861; by November many people thought that the army must be ready; but McClellan refused to move. The Joint Committee of Congress was set up in December, and it increased the pressure upon Lincoln to urge McClellan to move. But no persuasion from Lincoln could achieve this object. McClellan snubbed Lincoln; he avoided him; he began to pick quarrels with the government.

At this stage Lincoln took a step which seems surprisingly naïve but which probably achieved its object. He issued a "General War Order" that a forward movement was to be made by the army of the Potomac and the western armies on February 22, 1862. It was an extreme step. It seems to have aroused McClellan to some action, and no doubt that is what Lincoln wanted. In fact, however, no forward move was made on February 22, and the Congressional Committee was anxious that Lincoln should dismiss McClellan. But McClellan had conceived the idea of the Peninsular Campaign and Lincoln was prepared to trust him, if only he would get ahead with something. Lincoln had a belief in McClellan, and that belief was justified. McClellan had undoubted professional gifts as a soldier, and his way of making war, by slow and thorough preparation for one stupendous blow, is perhaps America's most successful way of making war. But it is a method which imposes an enormous task upon the civilian Commander-in-Chief in a democratic country, the task of maintaining the morale and the patience of the nation while the blow is prepared. This was Lincoln's task, and it is fair to say that McClellan seemed to have no knowledge of it and no sympathy with it.

In the Peninsular Campaign Lincoln's intervention was most noticeable, and it may well be that it served to handicap McClellan and to assist his failure. No sooner had McClellan set off, than Lincoln, yielding to pressure and advice in Washington, ordered McDowell and his corps to guard Washington. McClellan had counted upon having them with him.

There has been a great controversy about the responsibility for the failure of the Peninsular Campaign. On the whole it seems that McClellan was given good support by the government, and that where there were misunderstandings and quarrels, McClellan himself must take a larger share of the responsibility. But there remains the fact of Lincoln's intervention to withhold the forces under McDowell. Here there had been a legitimate difference of opinion between Lincoln and McClellan. Lincoln had agreed to the Peninsular Campaign, with the stipulation that Washington must be covered. McClellan had accepted the stipulation. His view was that the best defence of Washington was a vigorous attack on Richmond, which would require the enemy to hold back all his forces to save the Confederate capital. After McClellan had left, Lincoln's advisers—and they were military men as well as politicians—persuaded him that he must ensure an actual army stationed around the District of Columbia. In the opinion of many military historians this caution of the President was excessive and unwise and his action should be considered as partly responsible for the failure of the Peninsular Campaign. It may be added perhaps that, even without McDowell's troops, McClellan, after two months of hard fighting, was before Richmond with 100,000 men in June, as against 70,000 on the Confederate side, under Lee.

After the failure of the Peninsular Campaign Lincoln began to change generals in fairly quick succession. When McClellan set out on the campaign he was replaced as General-in-Chief by Halleck, who had commanded in the west. Pope was placed in charge of the three armies around the area of Washington. But after the second battle of Bull Run, in August 1862, he was dismissed, and McClellan was called back. Once more the old struggle went on between those who proposed action and pursuit and McClellan with his plans for careful preparation and reorganisation. He won the victory of Antietam on September 17, 1862, but he allowed five weeks to elapse before he entered Virginia in pursuit of Lee, who had ample time to prepare to receive him. On November 7 Lincoln relieved him of his command and replaced him by Burnside, who in his turn was to fail. McClellan was finally out of the war. His one further act in the history of the Civil War was to stand in opposition to Lincoln in the Presidential election of 1864.

Lincoln's relations with McClellan none the less come near the model of what a civilian Commander-in-Chief's relations with his generals should be. He had picked a good soldier; he gave him his confidence; and he reserved to himself the right to be consulted, the right to encourage and the right to warn. His correspondence with McClellan shows him attempting to exercise all three rights. It was only when he felt that McClellan was not prepared to play his part, and when finally he came to doubt, in November 1862, after Lee's retreat, whether McClellan was really very much disturbed that Lee had got away, that he finally removed McClellan from his command.

Before Lincoln was to come to the end of his troubles

The Commander-In-Chief / 137

with his generals by the appointment of Ulysses S. Grant, he was to pass through the experience of the disasters associated with Burnside and Hooker, relieved at the last by the victory at Gettysburg under Meade. The most interesting document of this phase of the war, from the point of view of Lincoln's development as Commander-in-Chief, is the letter he wrote to Hooker upon his appointment to succeed Burnside. A passage deserves quotation:

"I have placed you at the head of the army of the Potomac. Of course I have done this upon what appears to be sufficient reasons, and yet I think it best for you to know that there are some things in regard to which I am not quite satisfied with you. I believe you to be a brave and skilful soldier, which of course I like. I also believe you do not mix politics with your profession, in which you are right. You have confidence in yourself, which is a valuable, if not an indispensable quality. You are ambitious, which, within reasonable bounds, does good rather than harm; but I think that during General Burnside's command of the army you have taken counsel of your ambition and thwarted him as much as you could, in which you did a great wrong to the country, and to a most meritorious and honorable brother officer. I have heard, in such a way as to believe it, of your recently saying that both the Army and the Government needed a Dictator. Of course it was not for this, but in spite of it, that I have given you the command. Only those generals who gain successes can set up dictators. What I now ask of you is military success, and I will risk the dictatorship. The Government will support you to the utmost of its ability, which is neither more nor less than it has done and will do for all commanders. I much fear that the spirit which you have aided to infuse into the army, of criticising their commander and withholding confidence from him, will now turn upon you. I shall assist you as far as I can, to put it down. Neither you nor Napoleon, if he were alive again, could get any good out of an army while such a spirit prevails in it. And now beware of rashness. Beware of rashness, but with energy and sleepless vigilance go forward and give us victories."

So far had Lincoln developed. But with this there went still that spirit which had led him to say of McClellan's behaviour towards him that he would "hold General McClellan's stirrup for him if he will only win us victories."

After the disaster of 1863 came the appointment of Grant at the beginning of 1864 and the working out of that great co-ordinated campaign in west and east which was to win the war for the Union. Lincoln had not met Grant until the latter came to Washington in March 1864, to take up his appointment as Lieutenant-General, a rank not held since Washington and requiring an act of Congress to legalise it. Grant approached Lincoln cautiously, but soon a complete confidence came to exist between the two, and Lincoln's letter to Grant gives some sign of this:

"Not expecting to see you again before the Spring campaign opens, I wish to express in this way my entire satisfaction with what you have done up to this time so far as I understand it. The particulars of your plans I neither know or seek to know. You are vigilant and self-reliant, and, pleased with this, I wish not to obtrude any constraints or restraints upon you. While I am very anxious that any great disaster or capture of our men in great numbers shall be avoided, I know these points are less likely to escape your attention than they would be mine. If there is anything wanting which is within my power to give, do not fail to let me know it. And now, with a brave army and a just cause, may God sustain you."

For the remainder of the war Lincoln and his chief soldier were in accord and there were no examples of that intervention which, up to the end of 1863, provides the chief evidence upon which to base an estimate of Lincoln's work as Commander-in-Chief.

To estimate his work is difficult because so much controversy has surrounded his relations with his generals. But it may be asserted here, as an opinion to which many writers no doubt will take exception, that Lincoln did not as a rule overstep the bounds which should surround the activity of a civilian Commander-in-Chief. He did not take on more than he should. Within the sphere appropriate to him he was at first hesitant and ill-advised; he was also inevitably ill-informed. But characteristically he began to learn. He read books about strategy and the history of war after the first battle of Bull Run. And he was ready to converse with anybody who had something to tell him. He had sense and intelligence and constancy and patience—all invaluable qualities for the civilian Commander-in-Chief, and he used them all to the full. Some of his biographers speak of him as the greatest strategist of the war. That is going much too far. What is easier to maintain is what was said by Frederick L. Paxson in *The American Civil War*: "His disposition and attitude were exactly what ought to be aimed at by the political leader charged with the conduct of a war. Respectively he chose generals, placed full confidence in them, saw them fail, and felt forced to intervene with his amateur strategy."

No picture of Lincoln as Commander-in-Chief is complete which omits to mention his grief at the loss of life which accompanied the war and of the suffering, misery, squalor and foulness which were the lot of the wounded and the prisoners on both sides. One of his hardest tasks was the consideration of the death sentences imposed by court martial on those who had deserted or spied or broken some serious regulation in the military code. He pardoned too many of them for the happiness of his generals, though he could be stern at times. His visits to hospitals and battlefields imposed a great strain upon him; he frequently wept and his habitual melancholy was deepened. Sometimes it forced him to a seemingly callous display of humour or insensitiveness, but it was too much feeling, not too little, that caused it. At other times his feelings found expression in a short speech or a letter. The Gettysburg oration is the supreme example. But here is the letter he wrote to Mrs. Bixby, of Boston:

"Executive Mansion, November 21, 1864.

"DEAR MADAM,—I have been shown in the files of the War Department a statement of the Adjutant-General of Massachusetts that you are the mother of five sons who have died gloriously on the field of battle.[2] I feel how weak and fruitless must be any words of mine which should attempt to

[2] It proved otherwise, Mrs. Bixby had lost only two sons. But Lincoln did not know of this when he wrote.

beguile you from the grief of a loss so overwhelming. But I cannot refrain from tendering to you the consolation that may be found in the thanks of the Republic they died to save. I pray that our heavenly Father may assuage the anguish of your bereavement, and leave you only the cherished memory of the loved and lost, and the solemn pride that must be yours to have laid so costly a sacrifice upon the altar of freedom.

"Yours very sincerely and respectfully,

"ABRAHAM LINCOLN."

Chapter 10

The Head of the Government

> "And one most lonely man in a drafty White House
>   Whose everlasting melancholy runs
>   Like a deep stream under the funny stories."
>   STEPHEN VINCENT BENÉT: *John Brown's Body.*

THE OFFICE OF President of the United States is often compared with that of Prime Minister of the United Kingdom. Each is head of the government, each has a Cabinet whose members he appoints and dismisses. Yet the positions differ so much that it is better not to think of these resemblances. The President holds office for a fixed term of four years and can be removed only by impeachment—a process of trial initiated by the House of Representatives and carried out before the Senate. It has been adopted once only in relation to a President, and then unsuccessfully, in the case of Andrew Johnson, Lincoln's successor. The Prime Minister, on the other hand, has no fixed term of office; he holds office so long as the House of Commons supports him. The President may not be a member of Congress; the Prime Minister must be a member of Parliament, and usually nowadays of the lower House. And finally, the President's Cabinet is not a Cabinet in the English sense. In England Cabinet Ministers are Members of Parliament, and they form a team under the leadership of the Prime Minister. In the United States Cabinet Ministers are political heads of departments, but they may not be members of Congress; they are not a team; they owe obedience to the President alone; they are under his control. Not all Presidents have thought it necessary to call their Ministers together regularly in a Cabinet meeting, as Lincoln did.

What the American Cabinet is today is a result of the proceedings of a succession of Presidents since the Constitution began to work. To no President does it owe more than to Abraham Lincoln. He used to the full the powers which the Constitution gave him as chief executive, and he treated his Cabinet accordingly. It is worth while perhaps to recall the powers of the President as head of the government.

The Constitution expressly says that "the executive power shall be vested in a President of the United States of America." It is assumed that he will have officials to assist him, for it says, "He may require the opinion, in writing, of the principal officer in each of the executive departments, upon any subject relating to the duties of their respective offices." But he has not the sole power to appoint the officials. In this executive act he must have the advice and consent of the Senate. "Ambassadors, other public ministers and consuls, judges of the Supreme Court and all other officers of the United States" require the Senate's consent to the President's appointment, subject to the proviso that "Congress may by law vest the appointment of such inferior officers, as they think proper, in the President alone, in the courts of law and in the heads of departments." The President's powers in foreign affairs are controlled by a provision that he may make treaties with the advice and consent of the Senate, provided two-thirds of the Senators present concur. He has power to grant pardons. He has the duty to take care that the laws of the United States be faithfully executed.

All these powers Lincoln was ready to exercise to the full. And he was prepared also to use the power, granted him by the Constitution, to give to Congress from time to time information on the state of the Union and to recommend to their consideration such measures as he judged necessary and expedient. But he thought that the President should not interfere unduly with Congress. On his journey to Washington as President-elect he said in a speech at Pittsburgh: "My political education strongly inclines me against a very free use of any of these means by the executive to control the legislature of the country. As a rule, I think it better that Congress shall originate as well as perfect its measures without external ties."

And it is true that, on the whole, he adhered to this view. It must be remembered that his conception of the extent of the President's own inherent powers was liberal, as a study of his work as Commander-in-Chief has shown, so that inevitably he presented Congress with *faits accomplis* which it might regard as an invasion of its own proper sphere. Where legislation was concerned, however, Lincoln confined himself to a strong recommendation, and even in this field it is noteworthy that very little legislation was initiated or carried through by the President. And when Congress in 1864 passed an act on the subject of reconstruction contrary to Lincoln's own advice and plans, he did not veto the bill. Instead he put it in his pocket, neither vetoing it nor approving it. Since Congress adjourned within ten days of presenting this bill to the President, by the terms of the Constitution the bill lapsed. But in a proclamation issued soon after, Lincoln agreed to regard the procedure outlined in the bill as appropriate and to consider it, along with his own proposed procedure, as fit to be put into operation. Similarly he was careful to leave to Congress its right to determine whether Representatives and Senators from rebel states should sit in the Houses, while he himself claimed a right to decide what governments in rebel states should be recognised.

This is not to say that Lincoln's relations with Congress were harmonious or that he liked to work with Congress. On the contrary, he liked to work apart from Congress. He tried to mark off his own executive department and keep within it. But here Congress disputed with him about the extent of his powers, and endeavoured to control him. And, in any case, the Constitution was against him. For although it separates the executive from the legislature to some extent, the separation is not complete. The laws which the President must enforce are the laws of Congress. He may veto its bills, but two-thirds of Congress may override the veto. He relies upon Congress for appropriation of money. He cannot make appointments without senatorial approval.

On the whole Lincoln was not successful with Congress. He neglected Congress. We have seen how at the outset of the Civil War he saw no need to summon Congress at once. "His chief effort," says Professor Randall, "to bring about a reform by legislative act—his scheme for emancipation of the slaves with Federal compensation—resulted in mere paper approval by Congress; it was never carried to the point of application. On the other hand, Congress passed several measures, such as the West Virginian Bill and the second Confiscation Act, of which Lincoln disapproved, but which he nevertheless signed. . . . Lincoln, in fact, seemed to prefer a legislative recess; he regarded Congress often as an embarrassment. Finding himself opposed in House or Senate by a powerful element (the "Jacobins" or Radicals) within his own party, he yielded to them where necessary, sinking his own preferences in so doing and using his well-tempered tact to prevent them from taking authority too much out of his hands. Meanwhile far-reaching acts of executive authority were performed in disregard of the legislative branch."

This aroused the hostility of Congress. And it is fair to say that much of the trouble which Lincoln's successor was to undergo in his relations with Congress, leading at last to its attempt to remove him by impeachment, had begun during the régime of Lincoln and to a large extent from his two principles of firstly, enlarging the extent of the executive powers, and secondly, of exercising that power so far as possible in isolation.

On the executive side itself Lincoln showed a similar desire to act alone. Cabinet meetings were held, but they were, according to Gideon Welles, Lincoln's Secretary of the Navy, "infrequent, irregular and without system." "Little was before the Cabinet, which of late can hardly be called a council. Each department conducts and manages its own affairs, informing the President to the extent it pleases." "Stanton (Secretary of War) does not attend one half of the Cabinet meetings. When he comes he communicates but little information. Not infrequently he has a private conference with the President in the corner of the room, or with Seward (the Secretary of State) in the library." "The President did not join us today in Cabinet. He was with the Secretary of War and General Halleck, and sent word there would be no meeting. That is wrong, but I know no remedy."

Lincoln's Cabinet was inevitably ill-assorted. Presidents have seldom an absolutely free hand in appointing their Ministers. Party interests, states' interests and campaign pledges all tie their hands to some extent. In Lincoln's case there were two campaign pledges in which he had no part personally, but which his supporters had given. Simon Cameron, of Pennsylvania, had been promised Cabinet office in return for swinging his state's support to Lincoln at the Republican Convention, and Caleb Smith had been given a similar promise in return for the support of Indiana. Lincoln appointed Cameron to be Secretary of War and Caleb Smith to be Secretary of the Interior. Seward was appointed Secretary of State because of his outstanding position in the Republican party; Chase was appointed Secretary of the Treasury because of his prominence as anti-slavery leader, his ability and his rivalry to Lincoln as a Presidential candidate in his own party. But the appointment of both men— Seward and Chase—was clearly justifiable on grounds of ability. Welles was made Secretary of the Navy. He was chosen as a New Englander—Connecticut was his state. Edward Bates, of Missouri, as Attorney-General, and Montgomery Blair, of Maryland, as Postmaster-General, represented border slave states. Lincoln tried to get a representative of the lower South, but he failed.

On the whole Lincoln's Cabinet was abler than that of Jefferson Davis. In Chase, Seward and Welles he had men of first-rate ability. His weakest appointment was Cameron, who had no administrative ability to compensate for his skill as a mere politician. But in 1862 it was possible for Lincoln to move Cameron out of the Cabinet by appointing him as Minister to Russia. He appointed in his place Edward M. Stanton, a Democrat and a member of President Buchanan's Cabinet, a leading lawyer who had snubbed Lincoln when, in 1855, Lincoln appeared as his assistant counsel in an important legal case.

Lincoln's peculiar gift for acting alone and for holding on tenaciously in the midst of vexatious lobbying is well illustrated from the appointment of his Cabinet. He told Gideon Welles that when, on the night of his election as President, he came out of the telegraph office at Springfield, he had decided upon the membership of his Cabinet. After four months of debate and pressure, he appointed in March 1861 substantially the Cabinet he had decided on in November 1860. Of his final seven, four—Seward, Chase, Bates and Blair—were his personal choice; one, Welles, was suggested by Hannibal Hamlin, the Vice-President; and two, as

I have said, were already fixed for him—Cameron and Smith —by his party managers at the Chicago Convention. If we look at the party affiliations of the seven, we notice that Lincoln held the balance carefully. Three were former Whigs —Seward, Smith and Bates—and four were former Democrats—Chase, Cameron, Blair and Welles. The new Republican party was a fusion of Whigs and Free Soil Democrats. Lincoln saw to it that both elements were represented. And when a Whig friend said to him that he had given the Democrats a majority in the Cabinet, Lincoln reminded him that he himself would be in the Cabinet. When it came to choosing Cameron's successor, Lincoln acted alone once more and chose in Stanton, not a former Democrat, but an actual Democrat, the first to be admitted to office in his Cabinet.

Lincoln's supreme example of solitary action came with the formulation and announcement of his policy upon emancipation. He produced the draft of his proclamation at a Cabinet meeting on July 8, 1862. He had informed two members of the Cabinet—Seward and Chase—beforehand of what he intended to do. When he presented the draft, he informed his Cabinet that he was not asking their aproval, but he would be interested to have their opinions. He certainly took notice of what one of them said—Seward—and decided to postpone making the proclamation until a victory had been achieved. When the time arrived, he showed the final draft of the proclamation to the Cabinet and again remarked that he did not ask their approval. It was his own affair, and he chose to act throughout on an issue of first-rate importance in policy on his own responsibility.

Lincoln had made it clear upon his assumption of office that he would reserve to himself the power of ultimate control over policy. His Secretary of State, Seward, was a man of great ability and confidence, and had had far greater experience of national politics than Lincoln. He thought that he could manage Lincoln, who had great confidence in him. When, therefore, weeks passed after Lincoln's inauguration and the President still took no decisive action to deal with the growing crisis in the Union, Seward took the initiative and presented to Lincoln a memorandum entitled "Thoughts for the President's Consideration." It was dated April 1,

1861, and began: "We are at the end of a month's administration, and yet without a policy, either domestic or foreign." It went on to sketch a policy of great vigour. "I would maintain every fort and possession in the South. I would demand explanations from Spain and France, categorically at once. I would seek explanations from Great Britain and Russia, and send agents into Canada, Mexico and Central America, to arouse a vigorous spirit of independence on this continent against European intervention. And if satisfactory explanations are not received from Spain and France, would convene Congress and declare war against them." There was the policy. But next Seward came to the central question. "Whatever policy we adopt," he said, "there must be an energetic prosecution of it. For this purpose it must be somebody's business to pursue and direct it incessantly. Either the President must do it himself, and be all the while active in it, or devolve it on some member of his Cabinet. Once adopted, debates on it must end, and all agree and abide. It is not my especial province. But I neither seek to evade nor assume responsibility."

Here was an unmistakable hint from the Secretary of State that in his view Lincoln was unlikely to show the capacity to act with sufficient strength and vigour to cope with the crisis and that he should devolve his functions upon Seward himself. It may seem a cool and presumptuous proposal. But it is to be remembered that Lincoln's inactivity was exasperating to his colleagues. Seward's protest had some justification in it, the more so in that it probably assisted to force Lincoln into action.

Lincoln's response is interesting. He replied the same day. He ignored the personal criticisms in the memorandum, except to remark that the policy he was pursuing was one to which Seward had given his assent at the outset. And he concluded that, so far as the energetic prosecution of policy was concerned, "if this must be done, I must do it. When a general line of policy is adopted, I apprehend there is no danger of its being changed without good reason or continuing to be a subject of unnecessary debate; still upon points arising in its progress I wish, and suppose I am entitled to have, the advice of all the Cabinet." This was a rebuke to Seward. But he took it well. Neither he nor Lincoln appears to have divulged the affair to any other person nor to have referred to it again. Lincoln's secretary Nicolay saw the correspondence, and he published it only after the two men were dead.[1]

The incident illustrates Lincoln's strength and weakness as head of the government. He had strength, but not continuing energy. The first-rate administrator needs both. A great American, Alexander Hamilton, writing of the Presidency in *The Federalist* in 1788, had said: "Energy in the Executive is a leading character in the definition of good government." Lincoln was ready in some things to act alone and in opposition to his Cabinet. But he was not an omnipresent supervisor of the administration. He left it to his separate secretaries to control their own departments. As a result there was inter-departmental warfare; there was a lack of co-ordination; and there was delay.

One further incident involving Seward illustrates Lincoln's strength and weakness as an administrator. On April 9, 1861, Lincoln decided, without consulting his Cabinet, that two expeditions should be sent, one to relieve Fort Sumter and the other Fort Pickens. In the execution of the plans a serious muddle occurred.[2] The President authorised the Secretary of the Navy, Welles, to issue orders assigning a powerful warship, the *Powhatan*, to the Sumter expedition. But Seward, who thought that the relief of Fort Pickens was more important, drew up an order transferring the *Powhatan* to the Fort Pickens expedition. This order he placed before Lincoln, who signed it without reading it. Seward was, of course, interfering with a department that did not concern him, but if one admits that he was entitled to draw the President's attention to the subject, the President should have troubled to read the order placed before him. When Lincoln discovered what he had done, he overruled Seward and ordered him to restore the ship to the Sumter expedition. Seward sent the new order, but sent it in his own name. The

[1] The document is contained in the Lincoln papers formerly in the custody of Robert Lincoln, now in the Library of Congress, and made available to the public July 26, 1947.

[2] See pp. 92–93.

commander of the *Powhatan* refused to obey it because it conflicted with his previous orders, which were in the President's name. So the *Powhatan* did not sail with the Sumter expedition, and without it the expedition could not succeed.

Commenting on this incident, Professor Randall says: "In this extraordinary episode one sees cross-purposes in the Lincoln cabinet, administrative looseness in the sending of a dispatch which the President signed without reading, struggle for authority on the part of Seward, interference by one department with the affairs of another, confusion among naval officers when confronted with conflicting orders, and inefficiency (some might say audacity) in having a peremptory order of the President sent out in the name of a cabinet secretary."

Lincoln had little interest or belief in "administration." He left that to his Ministers and their departments. As a man from the frontier, he thought bureaucracy was unnecessary and over-elaborate. He had had no administrative experience, so that he was not aware even of the virtues of a bureaucracy. Had it not been for the skill and devotion of his two personal private secretaries, Nicolay and Hay, the conduct of his own office work would have been chaotic. Hay wrote of him: "He was extremely unmethodical: it was a four years' struggle on Nicaloy's part and mine to get him to adopt some systematic rules. He would break through every regulation as fast as it was made. Anything that kept the people themselves away from him he disapproved—although they nearly annoyed the life out of him by unreasonable complaints and requests. He wrote very few letters. He did not read one in fifty that he received." He conducted a good deal of business with his youngest and favourite son, Tad, sitting upon his knee or lying about in the office.

Yet, with all this, Lincoln could assume control when he wanted to and where he wanted to. Some of his most striking interventions came in the State Department, particularly in the early days of the war. It is of interest to English readers to see how Lincoln's influence was decisive, on the American side, in keeping peaceful relations with England. Not that Lincoln had any strong affection for England. It is true that he was originally of English descent: on his father's side his ancestry has been traced back to Samuel Lincoln, a weaver's apprentice who emigrated from Hingham in Norfolk in 1637 and settled at Hingham, Massachusetts. But in the years of sojourning and travelling from Massachusetts to Pennsylvania, to Virginia, to Kentucky and then on to Indiana and Illinois, the Lincolns had become Americans, and Abraham Lincoln was essentially an American. He thought of England as an aristocratic country in contrast to America as a democracy, and he was ready to believe—and there was evidence for it—that many influential Englishmen favoured the cause of the South. Gladstone's statement already quoted is one example of it. None the less, Lincoln was wise enough to see that no good could come to the Union's cause by alienating the greatest naval Power in the world of that time. His actions in a crisis were, therefore, unfaltering.

Soon after the outbreak of the Civil War, Britain declared itself a neutral as between the contending parties, both of which it recognised as "belligerents." This was disappointing and irritating to the Union, which regarded the South not as an independent state but as rebels, and it thought that British action in speaking of "neutrality" tended to elevate the Southern goverment into an independent state. Moreover, certain agents of the South had gone to England to obtain assistance, and they had been unofficially in contact with the British government. Seward decided that a strong protest should be made to the British government against this action, and he drafted a dispatch for the United States Minister in London, Mr. Adams. It contained many vigorous and provocative passages. It asserted that if Britain should come to recognise the South as an independent state "we shall from that hour cease to be friends and become once more, as we have twice before been forced to be, enemies of Great Britain." And the dispatch concluded with a passage which warned Britain and accused her of provoking the Civil War.

The dispatch was shown to Lincoln. He worked through it carefully. He cut out certain provocative passages; he watered down others. He deleted in particular the passage just quoted, putting a ring round it and writing "Leave out." And he advised that the whole of the final paragraph be deleted and that these words, addressed to the United States Minister, should be added: "This paper is for your own guidance only and not [to] be read or shown to anyone." The sequel was interesting. Seward adopted the suggestion that the dispatch should be for Mr. Adams' guidance only, but he retained his final paragraph. It was innocuous, not to say futile, once it became clear that the Minister alone would read it.

The great crisis in the Union's relations with Britain came in 1861 over what is called the *Trent* affair. A Union warship stopped a British merchant ship, the *Trent*, which was carrying two Southern envoys to Europe, one James M. Mason, on his way to Britain, and the other John Slidell, on his way to France, and carried off the two envoys. This incident cause great indignation in Britain and there was talk of war. On the British side Palmerston's threatening dispatch to the Union government was greatly modified at the suggestion of the Prince Consort and Queen Victoria; on the American side Lincoln intervened to ensure moderation. As he said, he did not want "two wars on his hands at one time." He was careful to make no public reference to the incident. In his Annual Message to Congress on December 3, 1861, nothing was said about it, though it was a topic everyone was discussing. Lincoln himself was ready to propose arbitration. In the end, by his careful and unobstrusive handling of the situation, it was possible for the United States to release the Southern envoys with a good grace. In the course of the incident it became clear to Lincoln and the Union too that there were forces in Britain that stood on their side, and in particular John Bright and Richard Cobden stood out as friends of the Union. There were to be further incidents after this which caused difficulty between Britain and the Union. But at no time did Britain recognise the Confederacy; after 1862 she furnished no warships to the South; and if we contrast Britain's attitude with that of France under Napoleon III, which took advantage of the Union's plight to support the invasion of Mexico and the placing of a Hapsburg upon the throne there, we shall feel that the British record is relatively good, if not indeed sympathetic.

Yet as the war progressed British admiration for Lincoln increased. It is true that in 1861 Lord John Russell said: "President Lincoln looming in the distance is a still greater peril than President Buchanan." Even Richard Cobden, who saw Lincoln at Springfield just after his election, wrote of him as "a backwoodsman of good sturdy common sense, but . . . unequal to the occasion." Lord Lyons, the British Minister at Washington, called Lincoln "a rough farmer— who began life as a farm labourer—and got on by a talent for stump speaking." In fairness to these critics, it is right to say that Lincoln grew with his tenure of the Presidency. The powers and the opportunities that the headship of the government gave him brought out his great resources of strength and steadfastness. One of his rewards was the address he received at the end of 1862 from the working men of Manchester, who suffered great privations through the Civil War because of the shortage of cotton for the mills of Lancashire, but who declared themselves in favour of the cause of the Union. In his reply to their address Lincoln concluded with these words: "Whatever misfortune may befall your country or my own, the peace and friendship which now exist between the two nations will be, as it shall be my desire to make them, perpetual."

Perhaps one of the best indications of Lincoln's attitude to his Cabinet is contained in the story told of a debate at a Cabinet meeting in which all the members were opposed to him. Lincoln is alleged to have said: "Seven nays, one aye, the ayes have it." It is worth recording too that Lincoln made full use of the power of patronage which was— and still is, though to a less extent—the acknowledged instrument by which an American President influenced Congress and politicians. Lincoln was not above the full use of these powers. He had in his gift a vast patronage, including quite minor offices, such as postmasterships in small villages. In his appointments to the most important offices— such as Cabinet posts—the Constitution required that he obtain the consent of the Senate. For the inferior offices custom required that he should consult the Senators and Representatives of his own party from the locality concerned. In this way he could ensure their goodwill, and he could ensure further that the officers of the United States were loyal to the administration, a qualification of transcendent importance at that critical time. In these minor posts, therefore, he used his power of patronage to provide the greatest measure of support for his administration. In the highest posts he followed wider principles in some cases. The appointment of Stanton was an example where mere party and personal considerations were put aside.

The whole business of patronage, of dealing with office-seekers, was arduous and vexatious. "There are too many pigs for the tits," he said. At the beginning of his first term of office, someone saw Lincoln looking especially worried. "What is the matter, Mr. President?" he said. "Is there bad news from Fort Sumter?" "Oh, no," Lincoln replied, "it's the Post Office at Baldinsville." Appointments too could lead to disputes with members of the Cabinet. Chase, the Secretary of the Treasury, maintained that his recommendations for appointments under that department should prevail over the suggestions of local politicians. Lincoln could not, as a rule, accept this proposition. There was a series of four difficulties on this point in 1863–5. On the first occasion Chase had written out his resignation, but did not send it in; on the second he resigned, and Lincoln felt obliged to persuade him to withdraw it. Chase carried his point on the third occasion. On the fourth he prepared his resignation, and when he had once more carried his point, he sent it in. This time it was accepted. Yet it was Chase whom Lincoln nominated for the Chief Justiceship of the Supreme Court within six months of this date, in spite of their disputes and in spite of their rivalry for the Presidential nomination in 1864.

As head of the government Lincoln was, of course, the target for all criticism and complaint that anyone had to make against the administration. And he was the irresistible subject of the cartoonists' art; their representations varied from the savage ape to the benevolent father of his people. Perhaps the most interesting medium of criticism and comment on the war is found in the writings of the humorous authors of the time. The most famous of these was Artemus Ward, who published in May 1862 a work entitled *Artemus Ward*: *His Book*. He specialised in quaint spelling and phrases and in droll stories. Lincoln was very fond of his work and, as will be seen later, actually read it aloud to his Cabinet on a fateful occasion. It is interesting to notice that all the great American humorists of the time were on the side of the Union, and showed a remarkable understanding of Lincoln. Their support undoubtedly assisted the Union cause. There was Artemus Ward, whose real name was Charles Farrar Browne, and who was only twenty-eight when he published his book; there was David R. Locke, who called himself the Reverend Petroleum Vesuvius Nasby, and was a year older than Ward; and there was Robert H. Newell, also under thirty, who created Orpheus C. Kerr (a pun on the words Office-Seeker). Lincoln read these men with great delight and comfort, and they in their turn appear to have respected him. As Carl Sandburg says—and his account of these writers and of Lincoln's humour in the third volume of his *Abraham Lincoln: The War Years* is the classic treatment of this theme —"they shaded their foolery and colored their jests as if in the White House was one of their own, a fellow of the craft of clowning who nevertheless carried merit and dignity." It is not possible to appreciate Lincoln fully unless one reads these writers; they are more revealing than most learned studies. They help one to understand how it was possible for the following story to be told about the melancholy, sad man of the White House and to ring true:

"Two Quakeresses were travelling in a train, and one was heard to say to the other:

" 'I think Jefferson[3] will succeed.'

" 'Why does thee think so?'

" 'Because Jefferson is a praying man.'

" 'And so is Abraham a praying man.'

" 'Yes, but the Lord will think Abraham is joking.' "

And here is part of an Artemus Ward story which tells much truth by fiction of the ways, particularly the story-telling ways, of the head of the government. It is cast as an alleged interview with Lincoln:

[3] Meaning Jefferson Davis, the President of the Confederacy.

"I called on Abe. He received me kindly. I handed him my umbreller, and told him I'd have a check for it if he pleased. 'That,' sed he, 'puts me in mind of a little story. There was a man out in our parts who was so mean that he took his wife's coffin out of the back winder for fear he would rub the paint off the doorway. Well, about this time there was a man in an adjacent town who had a green cotton umbreller.'

"'Did it fit him well? Was it custom made? Was he measured for it?"

"'Measured for what?' said Abe.

"'The umbreller.'

"'Well, as I was sayin',' continued the President, treating the interruption with apparent contempt, 'this man sed he'd known that there umbreller ever since it was a parasol. Ha, ha, ha!'

"'Yes' sed I, larfin in a respectful manner, 'but what has this man with the umbreller to do with the man who took his wife's coffin out of the back winder?'

"'To be sure,' sed Abe, 'what was it? I must have got two stories mixed together, which puts me in mind of another lit——'

"'Never mind, Your Excellency. I called to congratulate you on your career, which has been an honest and a good one—unscared and unmoved by Secesh in front of you and Abbolish at the back of you—each one of which is a little wuss than the other if possible! . . .'

"I took my departer. 'Goodbye, old Sweetness!' sed Abe, shaking me cordyully by the hand.

"'Adoo, my Prahayrie flower!' I replied, and made my exit. 'Twenty five thousand dollars a year and found,' I soliloquised, as I walked down the street, 'is pretty wages for a man with a modist appytite, but I reckon that it is worth it to run the White House.'"

Chapter 11

The Emancipator of the Slaves

"If God reads
The hearts of men as clearly as He must
To be Himself, then He can read in mine
And has, for twenty years, the old, scarred wish
That the last slave should be for ever free
Here, in this country."
STEPHEN VINCENT BENÉT: *John Brown's Body.*

ONE OF THE MOST startling sentences that Lincoln uttered on the question of slavery is this: "What I do about slavery and the coloured race, I do because I believe it helps to save the Union; and what I forbear, I forbear because I do not believe it would help to save the Union." To so many people Lincoln's name is associated with the abolition of slavery in the United States that it must come as a shock to find that his object in the Civil War was "to save the Union, and not either to save or to destroy slavery." He held this as his policy, although he cherished an "oft-expressed personal wish that all men everywhere could be free."

It helps us to get proportions right, too, if we remember that Lincoln expressly denied the equality of white and black in the United States. He did not favour inter-marriage between the races, and he believed that the best solution was for the negroes to be transported to some other country and found a colony of their own. He told a deputation of educated negroes on August 14, 1862, that their presence in America caused them great suffering, but it caused the white people great suffering also on their account. He said: "Even when you cease to be slaves, you are yet far removed from being . . . on an equality with the white race. . . . It is better for us both . . . to be separated."

Lincoln asserted his policy consistently from the beginning. In his First Inaugural Address, before the war had begun, he quoted from one of his earlier speeches: "I have no purpose, directly or indirectly, to interfere with the institution of slavery in the states where it exists. I believe I have no lawful right to do so, and I have no inclination to do so." After the war began he had opportunities of maintaining this policy. In August 1861, Frémont, who had been Republican Presidential candidate in 1856, and whom Lincoln had appointed to command the Department of the West, determined to link the slavery question with the Civil War. He issued a proclamation on August 30 establishing martial law in Missouri and declaring that "the property, real and personal, of all persons in the state of Missouri who shall take up arms against the United States, or who shall be directly proven to have taken an active part with their enemies in the field, is declared to be confiscated to the public use; and their slaves, if any they have, are hereby declared free men." To many people this seemed a justifiable proclamation. What was the use of fighting a civil war and preserving the Union if at the same time slavery was to be preserved, slavery, the very cause of the struggle and disunion? What more reasonable than that the rebel states should lose their slaves? And was not this a shrewd military blow against them? Would it not reduce their sinews of war?

Lincoln immediately saw dangers in Frémont's proclamation. To begin with, he did not believe that it was justified by military necessity at that time. And, even more important, he saw that such a policy would lose the Union the support of those slave states which still adhered to it, and especially Kentucky, whose decision was still in the balance. He expressed his views to Frémont in a private letter. He said that "the liberating slaves of traitorous owners will alarm our Southern Union friends and turn them against us; perhaps ruin our rather fair prospect of Kentucky." He urged the general to modify his proclamation. But Frémont was unwilling and obliged the President himself to order the change. Frémont obtained popularity among anti-slavery men by this action; Lincoln was placed upon the defensive. Even his close friend Senator Browning felt unhappy about his policy and wrote to him to say so. Lincoln replied at length to justify his action.

He said that Frémont's proclamation "is purely political, and not within the range of military law or necessity." If the general needs the slaves, "he can seize them and use them, but when the need is past, it is not for him to fix their permanent future condition. That must be settled according to laws made by law-makers, and not by military proclamations." "So much as to principle. Now as to policy. No doubt the thing was popular in some quarters, and would have been more so if it had been a general declaration of emancipation." That is one side of the question, but the President must look at another. "The Kentucky legislature would not budge till that proclamation was modified; and General Anderson telegraphed me that on the news of General Frémont having actually issued deeds of manumission, a whole company of our volunteers threw down their arms and disbanded. . . . I think to lose Kentucky is nearly the same as to lose the whole game. Kentucky gone, we cannot hold Missouri, nor, as I think, Maryland. These all against us, and the job on our hands is too large for us."

These arguments have a special interest because, a year later, Lincoln himself, as Commander-in-Chief, was to issue a proclamation of emancipation on grounds of military necessity. Events pushed him in September 1862 to a policy which, in August 1861, he did not believe to be justified. But in the meantime Lincoln's policy was not purely negative. On the contrary he recommended and supported measures for the abolition of slavery by gradual methods in line with the proposals he had advocated in the early years of his political career. In 1861 he had an opportunity of supporting these methods in the small state of Delaware, a slave state still adhering to the Union cause. Lincoln made a proposal to the representatives of Delaware in Congress that the state legislature should adopt a scheme of gradual compensated abolition, by which the United States should pay to the state four hundred dollars for each slave in annual instalments spread over a period of thirty-one years, the state distributing the money to the individual owners. There were only 1,798 slaves in Delaware, but if this state could begin a movement of gradual and compensated emancipation, in co-operation with the Union government, Lincoln hoped that Maryland and other states might follow. But Delaware rejected the proposal by one vote in the state's Senate.

Lincoln next brought his proposal to the legislature of the United States itself. In a special message to the two Houses of Congress, on March 6, 1862, he recommended them to adopt the following joint resolution:

"That the United States ought to co-operate with any state which may adopt gradual abolishment of slavery, giving to such state pecuniary aid, to be used by such state, in its discretion, to compensate for the inconveniences, public and private, produced by such change of system."

Here was a moderate proposal, the proposal of a man who, as he said himself in this message, believes that "gradual, and not sudden emancipation is better for all." And it respected the claims of the states to regulate slavery within their own borders. The two Houses passed the joint resolution. This was the greatest success that Lincoln was to have in enlisting the support of Congress for his plan of compensated emancipation. But it was not followed up by any further Congressional action except in one small respect. In April 1862 Congress passed a bill for the immediate emancipation of the slaves in the District of Columbia, on payment to their owners of about three hundred dollars for each slave, and for the appointment of a commission to assess and award the compensation.

Lincoln did not cease to urge upon the loyal slave states the wisdom of his plan of gradual and compensated emancipation. A few days after sending his message to Congress he called together the representatives in Congress from these states and attempted to persuade them to commend this plan to their states. But no progress was made, and radical Abolitionists were very critical of the President's moderate measures, which, in their view, did nothing to decrease slavery, and, on the contrary, disheartened and alienated many supporters of the Union's cause in the war.

The radical Abolitionists were soon to have one more incident to excite their hopes and to irritate their feelings towards the President. In May 1862 another example of attempted emancipation by military order occurred. General Hunter, the Commander of the Department of the South, issued a military order on May 9 in these terms:

"Slavery and martial law in a free country are altogether

incompatible; the persons in these three states—Georgia, Florida and South Carolina—heretofore held as slaves are therefore declared forever free."

As soon as the President heard the news he acted at once to overrule the order. He asserted in a proclamation that the policy of the Union in regard to the emancipation of slaves had been declared by Congress in its joint resolution. It was gradual and compensated emancipation. He urged the slave states to accept these proposals for, he warned them, less attractive policies might come to be adopted in the future. "You cannot, if you would," he said, "be blind to the signs of the times."

And indeed it was this note of warning which was most significant about Lincoln's proclamation to annul General Hunter's order. He gave unmistakable hints that the slave states were being given a last chance. He made it clear that emancipation by reason of military necessity was not necessarily out of the question now. It was still true that no single military commander could take this action without the authority of the President. But, he added, "whether it be competent for me, as Commander-in-Chief of the army and navy, to declare the slaves of any State or States free, and whether, at any time, in any case, it shall have become a necessity indispensable to the maintenance of the government to exercise such supposed power, are questions which, under my responsibility, I reserve to myself, and which I cannot feel justified in leaving to the decision of commanders in the field." There is no longer the unequivocal assertion of the letter to Senator Browning, that the permanent future condition of slaves must not be settled by military proclamations, no longer the certainty that a President must not "make permanent rules of property by proclamation." On the contrary, these courses may be necessary. The President himself, as Commander-in-Chief, must decide. Meanwhile the slave states were urged to accept the Union's offer of compensated emancipation while there was still time.

But no encouraging response came. Lincoln had interviewed the Congressional representatives of the loyal slave states once more on July 12, 1862, and had urged his policy upon them. But to no avail. And so at last Lincoln determined upon a measure of emancipation upon the ground of military necessity. We can describe in his own words what led him to this decision. "Things had gone on from bad to worse," he said, "until I felt that we had reached the end of our rope on the plan of operations we had been pursuing; that we had about played our last card, and must change our tactics or lose the game. I now determined upon the adoption of the emancipation policy; and without consultation with, or the knowledge of, the Cabinet, I prepared the original draft of the proclamation, and after much anxious thought called a Cabinet meeting upon the subject. . . . I said to the Cabinet that I had resolved upon this step, and had not called them together to ask their advice, but to lay the subject matter of a proclamation before them, suggestions as to which would be in order after they had heard it read." Two members of the Cabinet had, in fact, been informed of his intentions a couple of days after his last interview with the representatives of the loyal slave states—the Secretary of State, Seward, and the Secretary of the Navy, Gideon Welles. To the remainder it was a surprise.

The policy adopted in the proclamation was not complete emancipation throughout the United States. It proposed to grant freedom to all persons held as slaves within any state or states wherein the constitutional authority of the United States was not practically recognised. The slaves of loyal states were not to be emancipated. This discrimination was naturally resented by radical Abolitionists. It could be justified only on grounds of expediency and of military necessity. The slave-owners of rebel states were to be deprived of their property as a means of defeating them. Moreover, due notice of emancipation was to be given. It was to take effect from January 1, 1863. Meanwhile the proclamation reiterated the President's intention to recommend to Congress once more "the adoption of a practical measure for tendering pecuniary aid to the free choice or rejection of any and all states which may then be recognising and practically sustaining the authority of the United States, and which may then have voluntarily adopted, or thereafter may voluntarily adopt, gradual abolition of slavery within such state or states."

The proclamation based itself upon military necessity. It

described emancipation as "a fit and necessary military measure" for prosecuting the war. And it was to give no temporary freedom. Slaves emancipated by its operation "shall then, thenceforward and forever be free." The President had come at last to "make permanent rules of property by proclamation," the course which, in his letter to Senator Browning of a year before, he had declared subversive of the government of the United States. Yet any other form of emancipation would have been ridiculous. What value to proclaim that slaves in the rebel states should be free "until the end of the Civil War and thereafter if Congress provides or if the Constitution be amended accordingly." Lincoln had decided upon the policy; its constitutionality would have to be decided later. Emancipation was necessary if the war was to be won. If the war were lost, that was an end of emancipation; if the war were won, emancipation might then become adopted as the basis of the Union by constitutional amendment.

Lincoln's Cabinet were ready to support the policy of his proclamation, though they differed about the best method of making it known. His Postmaster-General Blair, saw at once that the policy would certainly affect the Republican party adversely in the forthcoming Congressional elections; he thought they would lose. In the end the advice of the Secretary of State was accepted by the President, that the publication of the proclamation should be postponed until some victory of the Union forces. The war news had been bad. To announce the new policy at such a moment would suggest that the Union government had become desperate. The result was, said Lincoln, "that I put the draft of the proclamation aside . . . waiting for a victory."

The appropriate victory did not come until two months later, at Antietam. In the meantime the agitation of the Abolitionists did not cease. Lincoln had taken his decision, but he was not yet ready to announce it. It was during this time that he made the pronouncement with which this chapter opened. Horace Greeley, a strongly anti-slavery Republican, had published, on August 20, 1862, in the New York Tribune, of which he was editor, an open letter addressed to the President in which he reproached him for not acting more vigorously against slavery. Lincoln replied on August 22: "My paramount object in this struggle is to save the Union, and is not either to save or to destroy slavery. If I could save the Union, without freeing any slave, I would do it; and if I could save it by freeing all the slaves, I would do it; and if I could save it by freeing some and leaving others alone, I would also do that." Here was a cautious uncommunicative answer. But at least it did foreshadow to the Abolitionists that, if necessary, the President would be ready to act against slavery, and it did warn the slave states that if the war continued and they resisted, they must expect to risk the loss of their slaves.

On September 13, 1862, a deputation from four religious denominations of Chicago waited upon the President and urged a proclamation of universal emancipation. Again he found it necessary to speak of the objections to such a course and to conceal his own decision in the matter. His reply to the deputation contains a most thoughtful criticism of his intended course of action; it says all that can be said against the proclamation. But, having made these points, he admitted his right as Commander-in-Chief, in time of war, to emancipate slaves as a measure which might best subdue the enemy. "I have not decided against a proclamation of liberty to the slaves," he said, "but hold the matter under advisement." The deputation was not pleased.

Four days later, September 17, 1862, the battle of Antietam, began, and when it became clear that a victory for the Union might be claimed, Lincoln called his Cabinet together. They met on September 22. The President of the United States then read to them the following:

"In the Faul of 1856, I showed my show in Utiky, a trooly grate sitty in the State of New York.

"The people gave me a cordyal recepshun. The press was loud in her prases.

"1 day as I was givin a descripshun of my Beests and Snaiks in my usual flowry stile what was my skorn and disgust to see a big burly feller walk up to the cage containing my wax figgers of the Lord's Last Supper, and ceese Judas Iscarrot by the feet and drag him out on the ground. He then commenced fur to pound him as hard as he cood.

" 'What under the son are you abowt?' cried I.

"Sez he, 'What did you bring this pussylanermus cuss here fur?' and he hit the wax figger another tremenjis blow on the hed.

"Sez I, 'You egrejus ass, that airs a wax figger—a representashun of the false 'Postle.'

"Sez he, 'That's all very well fur you to say, but I tell you, old man, that Judas Iscarrot can't show himself in Utiky with impunerty by a darn site!' with which observashun he kaved in Judassis hed. The young man belonged to 1 of the first famerlies in Utiky. I sood him, and the Joory brawt in a verdick of Arson in the 3d degree."

This was a chapter from Artemus Ward's book, which the author had just sent to the President. The chapter was entitled "High-handed Outrage at Utica."

This humorous composition itself and Lincoln's reading of it at such a time outraged the feelings of the Secretary of War, Stanton, who was a serious and earnest man. So indeed was Abraham Lincoln, but a reading from Artemus Ward was the characteristic way in which he expressed and relieved his serious and earnest feelings. He followed his reading with a statement to the Cabinet that his mind was now made up. He did not ask for their advice; he knew their opinions already. He proposed now to publish the proclamation. Postmaster-General Blair again mentioned the adverse effect such an announcement might have on the elections. But the Cabinet approved. In any case, Lincoln had determined to make the proclamation, and he did so forthwith.

To some the proclamation came as the great moral justification of the war. Horace Greeley exclaimed on seeing the proclamation "Henceforth and forever we shall be free people." But he was obliged to admit later that it was in advance of public opinion. And the victories of the Democrats in some of the Northern states in the elections of the autumn, 1862, proved that Postmaster-General Blair had prophesied aright. Democrats were able to say that the war was a war against slavery, not a war for the Union. The Southern States were nerved to fight harder. And for the time being, of course, no practical change in the status of the slaves occurred. Emancipation must wait upon Northern victories and the occupation of rebel states.

But compensated emancipation was not thrown overboard. The President in his proclamation had expressed his intention of pressing on with his plan and had declared that emancipation under war powers was confined only to slaves in states actually in rebellion. What of those loyal slave states and those which might be induced to return to their former loyalty? It was necessary to provide for them. On December 1, 1862, therefore, a month before the Emancipation Proclamation was to be issued in final and effective form, the President, in his Annual Message to Congress, proposed that it should pass a joint resolution initiating a constitutional amendment. This amendment would grant compensation to every state which abolished slavery before 1900; it would secure freedom for ever to all slaves released by the chances of war, but would provide compensation to all loyal owners of such slaves; and it would authorise Congress to appropriate money for colonising slaves in foreign countries. Here was a plan, again gradual and compensated, to abolish slavery, and it offered to the rebel states an alternative to persisting with the war. Antietam had not been followed by further victories. The outlook was still dark. And Congress for the present made no response.

Lincoln's gradual progress towards the policy embodied in the proclamation of January 1, 1863, is most interesting to follow. It is best summarised, perhaps, in a passage from a letter he wrote to a friend in the middle of 1863, which is worth quoting as his own justification of what he did:

"I am naturally anti-slavery. If slavery is not wrong, nothing is wrong. I cannot remember when I did not so think and feel, and yet I have never understood that the Presidency conferred upon me an unrestricted right to act officially upon this judgement and feeling. It was in the oath that I took that I would, to the best of my ability, protect and defend the Constitution of the United States. I could not take the office without taking the oath. Nor was it my view that I might take an oath to get power, and break the oath in using the power. I understood, too, that in ordinary civil administration this oath even forbade me to practically indulge my primary abstract judgement on the moral question of slavery. I had publicly declared this many times, and in many ways. And I aver that, to this day, I have done no official act in mere deference to my abstract judgement and feeling on slavery. I did understand, however, that my oath to preserve the Constitution to the best of my ability impressed upon me the duty of preserving, by every indispensable means, that government, that nation, of which that Constitution was the organic law. Was it possible to lose the nation and yet preserve the Constitution? By general law, life and limb must be protected, yet often a limb must be amputated to save life; but a life is never wisely given to save a limb. I felt that measures otherwise unconstitutional might become lawful by becoming indispensable to the preservation of the Constitution, through the preservation of the nation. Right or wrong, I assumed this ground, and now avow it. I could not feel that, to the best of my ability, I had ever tried to preserve the Constitution, if, to save slavery or any minor matter, I should permit the wreck of government, country and Constitution all together. When, early in the war, General Frémont attempted military emancipation, I forbade it, because I did not then think it an indispensable necessity. When, a little later, General Cameron, then Secretary of War, suggested the arming of the blacks, I objected because I did not yet think it an indispensable necessity. When, still later, General Hunter attempted military emancipation, I again forbade it, because I did not yet think the indispensable necessity had come. When in March and May and July, 1862, I made earnest and successive appeals to the border states to favour compensated emancipation, I believed the indispensable necessity for military emancipation and arming the blacks would come unless averted by that measure. They declined the proposition, and I was, in my best judgement, driven to the alternative of either surrendering the Union and with it the Constitution, or of laying strong hands upon the colored element. I chose the latter."

Throughout the year 1863 Lincoln laboured to establish emancipation. He issued his proclamation upon reconstruction at the end of the year and made it clear that the new governments of former rebel states could be recognised only if they supported the Emancipation Proclamation. That was an essential part of his terms. Any government desiring recognition must include the support of emancipation in its oath. "While I remain in my present position," he said, "I shall not attempt to restrict or modify the Emancipation Proclamation; nor shall I return to slavery any person who is free by the terms of that proclamation, or by any of the acts of Congress. For these and other reasons, it is thought best that support of these measures should be included in the oath." Some progress was made in 1863 along these lines, and in 1864 a few states actually reorganised themselves with free constitutions—Arkansas adopted emancipation in January 1864, Louisiana in September 1864, while early in 1865 Tennessee, Missouri and Maryland adopted free constitutions.

Meanwhile the President did not cease to urge Congress to initiate a constitutional amendment. But the opposition was strong. A resolution proposing an amendment to the Constitution prohibiting slavery throughout the United States was passed by the Senate by the necessary two-thirds majority on April 8, 1864. But when it was considered by the House of Representatives, it failed to obtain the two-thirds majority. This constitutional requirement of a two-thirds majority was an additional obstacle to the President's wishes, and it increased the power of the minority of Democrats who were opposed to emancipation.

The Presidential election was to be held in 1864, and with it the Congressional elections. The Republican party adopted Lincoln as their candidate once more, and they inserted a plank in their platform in favour of a constitutional amendment abolishing slavery. With the success of the Republicans in the elections it became clear that the new Congress could be expected to pass a joint resolution in favour of amendment. But this new Congress, though elected in November 1864, could not meet until December 1865, under the provisions of the Constitution. The old Congress held office until March 1865, and it was this old Congress which met in December 1864 and to which the President addressed his Annual Message on December 6. He reminded them of their refusal to propose the amendment in April 1864, and of the verdict of the people on the emancipation issue in the elections of November 1864, and he advised them to reconsider their position.

Action soon followed. The resolution was brought up for discussion in the House of Representatives on January 6, 1865, and it was finally approved by the requisite majority on January 31.[1] It had now to go to the legislatures of the states, for it would not come into effect until approved by three-fourths of them. But three-fourths of which states? The loyal states only, or all the states, loyal and rebel? Lincoln himself appears to have thought that the better policy was to require three-fourths of all the states—their verdict would be "unquestioned and unquestionable." In the event it fell to Lincoln's successor, President Andrew Johnson, to decide this question, and he chose the course which Lincoln appears to have favoured. It was not until December 18, 1865, that Secretary of State Seward was able to announce that the amendment had received the support of the legislatures of twenty-seven states, three-fourths of the thirty-six states which then composed the Union.

The Amendment, the Thirteenth, runs:

"Neither slavery nor involuntary servitude, except as a punishment for crime whereof the party shall have been duly convicted, shall exist within the United States, or any place subject to their jurisdiction. Congress shall have power to enforce this article by appropriate legislation."

To Lincoln's great pride, Illinois, his own state, was the first to ratify the amendment. And among the twenty-seven were four—Virginia, Louisiana, Tennessee and Arkansas—in which he had seen initiated his own plans for reconstruction.

---

[1] As mentioned above, it had already passed the Senate on April 8, 1864.

Chapter 12

Reconstruction

"And the long work of binding up the wounds
  Not yet begun. . . ."
STEPHEN VINCENT BENÉT: *John Brown's Body*.

THE PERIOD OF American history which follows the conclusion of the Civil War is called the period of reconstruction. But the process of reconstruction had to begin before the Civil War ended. For one thing, it was necessary for the Union government to consider before the war was won what policy it intended to pursue towards the defeated states. When the Union was restored by force of arms, how should it be reconstructed? Secondly, it was necessary for the Union government to take decisions in cases where individual states were occupied by the Union forces before the final surrender and end of the war occurred. These decisions inevitably involved some policy, however provisional, about reconstruction. Clearly a most obvious duty rested upon those whose war aim was to preserve the Union to consider how best the Union could be reconstructed, how the forces which had led to discord and secession could be nullified and how people who had been fighting to be free from the United States could be made a part once more of the Union. It was a most difficult task. Reconstruction after any war is difficult, but after a civil war it is most difficult of all. In a war between separate countries what is needed at the end of the war is that the combatants should each recover their strength and health, but there is no question of uniting them together in a single state under one government. But in a civil war, in a war of secession, when union wins, the combatants have to be made once more into a united state.

Abraham Lincoln, from the beginning of his term as President, saw the problem of reconstruction ahead, the problem of remaking the Union. His life ended before the true period of reconstruction had really begun. But before

169

the war was over he had already made known his own principles of reconstruction and he had already put them into practice in a few states, where the Union had prevailed.

In the early stages of the war movements had occurred in two states, Missouri and Virginia, which made reconstruction possible without any intervention of the Union government. In Missouri a state convention, called in 1861, had refused to ratify the ordinance of secession which the legislature had passed. It organised a provisional state government, and it provided for the election of Representatives and Senators to the Congress of the United States. The President recognised the provisional government and Congress admitted the Representatives and Senators, and then by popular action within the state itself, Missouri was restored to its former relation to the Union. In Virginia the proceedings were more complicated. After the state seceded in 1861 a minority organised a new state government loyal to the Union, with Francis H. Pierpoint as its governor. Representatives and Senators were elected to Congress. The Union gave full recognition to these steps. Then, in 1862, a part of the state of Virginia was cut off and organised as a new state of West Virginia, loyal to the Union. This new state of West Virginia was admitted to the Union by Congress; its government was recognised, and Representatives and Senators were admitted. These proceedings involved a certain amount of legal fiction. For the Constitution provides that "no new state shall be formed or erected within the jurisdiction of any other state" without the consent of the legislature of the state concerned as well as of Congress. The consent of the legislature of Virginia had therefore to be obtained. Congress decided that the Pierpoint government and legislature should be treated as the lawful government and legislature of Virginia and that their consent was sufficient. Although its representatives in Congress continued to be recognised for some time, the Pierpoint administration had little authority. It was called the "vest-pocket government" because it was so small and ineffective.

Different problems were presented by states which had resisted the Union forces and had eventually been overrun. What steps should be taken to initiate a government there?

Were loyalists to be discovered and placed in power? Were rebels to be pardoned and trusted again? For the initial stages Lincoln followed the course of appointing military governors in the subjugated states. By the end of 1863 five of the seceding states—Virginia, North Carolina, Tennessee, Arkansas and Louisiana—were subjugated in whole or in part. So far as Tennessee was concerned, Congress had decided to allow Andrew Johnson, a Senator from the state, who was on the Union side, although his state had seceded, to retain his seat, and it admitted similarly into the House two Representatives from the state who were loyal. On March 5, 1862, Lincoln appointed Senator Andrew Johnson to be military governor of Tennessee. It was this Andrew Johnson who was elected Vice-President of the United States under Lincoln in the election of 1864 and who was to succeed, on Lincoln's death in 1865, to the overwhelming burdens of reconstruction. Here we find him introduced to these problems in his home state in 1862 by Lincoln's action. It is to be noticed that Lincoln took care to appoint, not some Northern Republican to the post, but a Southern Democrat, a man of the state itself.

In the other subjugated states military governors were similarly appointed, but it was only in Louisiana that representatives were elected and admitted to Congress. By the end of 1863, when Lincoln was to make a bold intervention upon the whole question of reconstruction, there were still no provisional state governments existing in any of these five subjugated states. The military governor was still in charge. Not that Lincoln desired this state of affairs to continue for long. He instructed his military governors to take all steps they could to encourage the people of their states to choose members for Congress and to set up a state government. But this government would be recognised upon conditions. And after the preliminary Emancipation Proclamation of September 22, 1862, one of Lincoln's conditions was the acceptance of this proclamation. For this reason he was obliged to refuse a proposal that the old constitution of Louisiana, which permitted slavery, should be revived. "For my own part," he wrote, "I think I shall not, in any event, retract the emancipation proclamation, nor, as executive, ever return to slavery any person who is freed by the terms of that proclamation, or by any of the acts of Congress." On the other hand, it was not within the power of the President to say whether persons elected to Congress by Louisiana under a slave constitution should be admitted to sit there. That was a matter for Congress.

The trend of Lincoln's thoughts on reconstruction was displayed from time to time as the problem arose in Louisiana. "What we do want," he said in 1862, "is the conclusive evidence that respectable citizens of Louisiana are willing to be members of Congress and to swear support to the Constitution and that other respectable citizens there are willing to vote for them and send them." But it must be a genuine thing. It must express the actual wishes of the people. "To send a parcel of Northern men here as representatives, elected, as would be understood (and perhaps really so) at the point of the bayonet, would be disgraceful and outrageous; and were I a member of Congress here, I would vote against admitting any such man to a seat."

When he came to speak of what sort of constitution Louisiana should draw up, he said on August 5, 1863: "I would be glad for her to make a new constitution recognising the emancipation proclamation and adopting emancipation in those parts of the state to which the proclamation does not apply." But he realised that there must be a gradual readjustment of the relation between the two races. So he goes on immediately to speak in practical terms of this: "And while she is at it, I think it would not be objectionable for her to adopt some practical system by which the two races could gradually live themselves out of their old relation to each other, and both come out better prepared for the new. Education for young blacks should be included in the plan." And a little later he wrote: "If a new state government acting in harmony with this government and consistently with general freedom, shall think best to adopt a reasonable temporary arrangement in relation to the landless and houseless freed people, I do not object; but my word is out to be for and not against them on the question of their permanent freedom."

Here were some main lines of the new Union. Moderation marks some of them. Generosity indeed marks Lincoln's terms towards the rebel states. All he asks is genuine repentance. If the people of the state say honestly that they wish to return to their old allegiance and give some simple proof of it, they will be accepted. But one hard condition is now attached which before September 22, 1862, might not have been there. Slavery must be abolished in the repentant states. He has committed himself to it now. Mere allegiance to the Union is not enough. Slavery must go. This was a drastic decision, though unavoidable once the Emancipation Proclamation was out. But its consequences, of course, were serious. If the seceding states must abolish slavery as the price of returning to the Union, what was to happen in those loyal states where slavery had not been abolished? Must it not go from there too? We have seen that Lincoln thought that it should, though he had no power to force its disappearance. It is easy to see, however, that by his adoption of emancipation as a principle of reconstruction in the seceded states, he had taken his stand against all those still within the Union who favoured the retention of slavery.

Towards the close of 1863, with military governors in control of the five states of Virginia, North Carolina, Tennessee, Arkansas and Louisiana, and with only two of them—Tennessee and Louisiana—represented in Congress, Lincoln made his public intervention upon the problem of reconstruction. On December 8, 1863, he issued a proclamation of amnesty and reconstruction, and on the same date he explained his policy in his Annual Message to Congress. He enunciated the broad proposition that a full pardon would be issued to all persons—with certain exceptions—who had been in rebellion against the United States if they subscribed an oath to support the Constitution of the United States, to abide by and support all acts of Congress passed during the war with reference to slaves and all proclamations made by the President during the war with reference to slaves. With this proposal of amnesty there was joined a method of reunion. If, in any of the rebel states, persons to the number of one-tenth of the number of voters in the state in the Presidential election of 1860 were to be found willing, having taken the oath and acquired the pardon, to establish a state government upon principles consistent with the oath, the

President declared himself ready to recognise the government so established to be the government of the state and to maintain it according to the Constitution of the United States.

It was not a free pardon all round. There were exceptions. "All who are, or shall have been, civil or diplomatic officers or agents of the so-called Confederate Government; all who have left judicial stations under the United States to aid the rebellion; all who are or shall have been military or naval officers of the said so-called Confederate Government above the rank of colonel in the army or lieutenant in the navy; all who left seats in the United States Congress to aid the rebellion; all who resigned commissions in the army or navy of the United States and afterwards aided the rebellion; and all who have engaged in any way in treating coloured persons, or white persons in charge of such, otherwise than lawfully as prisoners of war, and which persons may have been found in the United States service as soldiers, seamen or in any other capacity"—to all these no pardon could be extended upon taking the oath.

Yet, even with these exceptions, the proposals were generous and simple. They were intended, as the proclamation itself said, "to present to the people of the states wherein the national authority has been suspended, and loyal state governments have been subverted, a mode in and by which the national authority and loyal state governments may be re-established within said states or in any of them; and while the mode presented is the best the Executive can suggest, with his present impressions, it must not be understood that no other possible mode would be acceptable." It was stressed that the proposals had no reference to loyal state governments, and that, whereas the President claimed the power to recognise new state governments, Congress alone could determine whether representatives elected in newly constituted states should be permitted to sit in the Houses. And finally it was indicated that any measure which a reconstituted state might adopt to provide temporarily for the freed people would not be objected to by the President, so long as it was consistent with their freedom. Proposals for contract labour which might prevent the freed slaves from wandering about workless and homeless would, for example, be approved. Complete freedom in practice, unregulated by law, would lead to chaos and disorder. Gradual emancipation in practice following upon complete emancipation in law once more commended itself to Lincoln.

The President expounded this plan in his message to Congress and urged it upon them with a variety of arguments. In its essentials it is seen to be in line with what he had proposed for Louisiana and the other subjugated states. There was pardon for those who honestly repented, but there must be also emancipation for the slaves.

The President's message was received by Congress with great enthusiasm. His secretaries John G. Nicolay and John Hay wrote: "The Executive Mansion was filled all day by a rush of Congressmen, congratulating the President and assuring him of their support in his wise and humane policy. The conservatives and radicals vied with each other in claiming that the message represented their own views of the crisis. . . . For a moment the most prejudiced Democrats found little to say against the message; they called it 'very ingenious and cunning, admirably calculated to deceive.' One representative, Francis W. Kellogg of Michigan, went shouting about the lobby of the House: 'The President is the only man. There is none like him in the world. He sees more widely and more clearly than any of us.' Horace Greeley said the message was 'devilish good.' Owen Lovejoy, the leading Abolitionist of the Western States, said: 'How beautiful upon the mountains are the feet of him that brought good tidings. I shall live to see slavery ended in America.'" "Men acted as though the Millennium had come," John Hay wrote in his diary. And this enthusiastic acceptance of his policy naturally pleased Lincoln. He set so great store upon the reconstruction of the Union that he can hardly have ever hoped that his proposals would receive such wide support.

But the beginnings of opposition were there. Henry Winter Davis, a Representative from Maryland, moved at once that the part of the President's message which referred to reconstruction should be referred to a special committee on the rebellious states. Davis was a man of high character, but he had come to dislike Lincoln intensely, and he was determined to resist the President's policy. He was made chairman of the special committee, and on February 15, 1864, he brought forward a plan of reconstruction opposed to Lincoln's. It rejected the notion that the rebellious states were still within the Union; it boldly declared them to be out of it. Congress was not prepared to accept this dogma without question, and the proposition was deleted from the bill. But the idea behind it, that the rebellious states had no rights under the Constitution, pervaded the rest of the bill. It rejected Lincoln's plan for "ten per cent" reconstruction. Instead it proposed that Congress should appoint a provisional governor in each of the states in rebellion, and that, after the military resistance to the United States should have been suppressed and the people sufficiently returned to their obedience to the Constitution and the laws, the white male citizens of the state should be enrolled, and then, when a majority of them had taken the oath of allegiance, the loyal people of the state should be entitled to elect delegates to a convention to re-establish a state government. This convention was required to insert into any constitution three provisions: first, a provision to prevent prominent civil or military officers of the Confederate government from voting for or becoming members of the legislature or governor; second, a provision that involuntary servitude is for ever prohibited and the freedom of all persons guaranteed in these states; and third, that no debts created by the rebel state government should be recognised or paid by the new state.

Further, as Davis objected to the exercise of Presidential power in this sphere, the bill contained provisions which ensured that no stage in the process of a state's readmission into the Union could be carried through finally without the approval of Congress. For he asserted that Congress alone had authority in the rebellious Territories. Therefore his bill provided that when a convention had adopted a constitution, or it had been ratified by the electors of the state, the President, after obtaining the assent of Congress, should by proclamation recognise the government so established and none other as the constitutional government of the state. Moreover, from the date of such recognition and not before, Congressmen and Presidential electors might be elected for the state. And finally the bill emancipated all slaves in the rebel states and declared any person hereafter holding any important office, civil or military, in the rebel service not to be a citizen of the United States.

With some of the provisions of the bill Lincoln obviously agreed, but its terms were more severe than those he had proposed. The proofs of repentance required of a rebel state were much more exacting. Moreover, he did not acknowledge that Congress, under the Constitution, had power to emancipate slaves in the rebel states. That power might belong to the executive as a war measure, but never to Congress. To this Davis replied that by rebellion the states were no longer states of the Union; they were outside the pale of the Constitution. Congress might legislate for them as it saw fit.

So effective was Davis's advocacy of this bill in the House that it passed on March 22, 1864, by seventy-three votes to fifty-nine. It was introduced into the Senate by Benjamin F. Wade, of Ohio, and it was finally passed. It was presented to the President for his signature on the last day of the session of Congress. Lincoln was not prepared to approve it. The bill would have nullified the attempts at reconstruction in Louisiana and Arkansas which he was then encouraging and supporting. At the same time he was not prepared to say that the method of reconstruction proposed in the bill was completely unacceptable. But it must not be prescribed as the only method. He was not prepared, therefore, to veto the bill or to sign it. He put it in his pocket and took no action. And by the terms of the Constitution the bill lapsed.

But he did not leave it at that. On July 8, 1864, he issued a proclamation, giving the text of the "Wade-Davis" Bill, as it was called, and explaining the reasons for his action. He said that he was unprepared, by a formal approval of the bill, to be inflexibly committed to any single plan of restoration, nor was he ready to set aside and hold for naught the free state constitutions and governments established in Arkansas and Louisiana. He denied the constitutional competence of Congress to abolish slavery in the states; he hoped that the constitutional amendment to abolish slavery would soon be passed. And he concluded by saying: "I am fully satisfied with the system of restoration contained in the bill as one very proper plan for the loyal people of any state choosing to adopt it, and I am, and at all times shall be, prepared to give the executive aid and assistance to any such people, so soon as military resistance to the United States shall have been suppressed in any such state, and the people thereof shall have sufficiently returned to their obedience to the Constitution and the laws of the United States, in which cases military governors will be appointed, with directions to proceed according to the bill."

It is important to remember that these measures were undertaken in the year of a Presidential election. Lincoln and his opponents and supporters were all fully aware of the implications of their actions. Lincoln's opponents could hope to discredit him in his party as lukewarm against slavery and as usurping the power of Congress. They could go further and insinuate that Lincoln's willingness to recognise state governments established by a mere 10 per cent of the people of the state was intended to ensure that he could obtain the Presidential votes of that state in the coming election. The reconstructed governments would be his creation and his pawns. Wade and Davis did not hesitate to make this charge in a manifesto issued on August 5, 1864, in the *New York Tribune*. "The President," they said, "by preventing this bill from becoming a law, holds the electoral votes of the rebel states at the dictation of his personal ambition." But in the outcome these charges failed to defeat Lincoln.

As it turned out, no states chose to come into the Union under the procedure proposed in the Wade-Davis Bill. Lincoln had continued, throughout the controversy, to encourage the reconstruction of Louisiana, Arkansas, Tennessee and Virginia upon the principles which he had adopted and had formulated in his proclamation of December 8, 1863, and his message to Congress of that date. In April 1864 a convention in Louisiana established a free-state constitution by 6,836 votes to 1,566 and, as the affirmative vote was more than 10 per cent of the voters in 1860, Lincoln recognised the new government. But Congressional recognition was withheld and there was uncertainty about Louisiana's future right up to the time of Lincoln's death. Thereafter the state underwent reconstruction under a system which Congress was later to establish.

In Arkansas also, although a constitution was adopted in March 1864, which Lincoln recognised, Congress refused to regard it as satisfactory and denied admission to its Representatives and Senators. Again, in Tennessee, after much dispute and struggle, a constitution was adopted which Lincoln recognised in February 1865, and again Congress refused to admit Representatives and Senators from the state either in the Thirty-Eighth Congress (1863–5) or in the Thirty-Ninth Congress, which assembled in December 1865, after the death of Lincoln and when a citizen of the state, Andrew Johnson, was by then President of the United States.

There is a final comment on the failure of Lincoln's plans for reconstruction. Virginia, whose "vest-pocket" government of Pierpoint had been recognised, was to have its representation denied admittance to the Thirty-Ninth and Fortieth Congresses, while in the Thirty-Eighth Congress it was represented in the Senate only. Its final reconstruction was to be undertaken by Congress without regard to the Pierpoint régime.

In the end Lincoln failed to put his plans of reconstruction into complete operation in any state. He was preoccupied with the subject right up to the last. When the news of the capitulation of the South reached Washington and the President was called upon to speak to the people, his reply was a careful defence of the Louisiana experiment. And his Second Inaugural Address on March 4, 1865, concluded with that great passage which epitomised his principles of reconstruction:

"With malice toward none; with charity for all; with firmness in the right, as God gives us to see the right, let us strive on to finish the work we are in, to bind up the nation's wounds; to care for him who shall have borne the battle, and for his widow, and his orphan—to do all which may achieve and cherish a just and lasting peace among ourselves, and with all nations."

Chapter 13

"Now he belongs to the Ages"

> "Until there is nothing there
> That ever knew a master or a slave
> Or, brooding on the symbol of a wrong,
> Threw down the irons in the field of peace."
> STEPHEN VINCENT BENÉT: *John Brown's Body*.

GENERAL ROBERT E. LEE surrendered at Appomattox Court House on April 9, 1865. President Jefferson Davis had fled with his Cabinet and his Congress. Lincoln said: "I should not be sorry to have them out of the country; but I should be for following them up pretty close, to make sure of their going."[1] He felt now a great relief; revenge which he had never invoked in war remained in peace almost beyond his comprehension. "Enough lives have been sacrificed," he said to his Cabinet on April 14. "We must extinguish our resentments if we expect harmony and union."

After the Cabinet meeting on April 14 Lincoln took a drive alone with his wife. He talked about the future. "Mary," he said, "we have had a hard time of it since we came to Washington, but the war is over, and with God's blessing we may hope for four years of peace and happiness, and then we will go back to Illinois and pass the rest of our lives in quiet." He had had a horrible and disturbing dream a few nights previously. He saw in his dream a dead man lying in state in the White House, and he asked, "Who is dead in the White House?" and a soldier answered: "The President. He was killed by an assassin." And he heard so loud a burst of grief from the crowd that he awoke from his dream. Lincoln had these disturbing dreams quite often. He told his wife of this one, and she and he tried to forget it. But it disturbed him.

[1] Davis was captured in Georgia on May 10; imprisoned in Fortress Monroe for two years; brought before the United States Circuit Court in Virginia to stand his trial for treason, but was released on bail and finally restored to the full rights of citizenship (except the right to hold office) at the end of 1868.

April 14 was Good Friday. It was not observed in the United States with the same general suspension of worldly activities as in Europe. Theatres, for example, were open as usual. Lincoln decided that he would attend Ford's Theatre in Washington that night to see a humorous piece called *Our American Cousin*. His wife and some friends accompanied him. They arrived late and were given an ovation. While they sat in their box and the play proceeded, John Wilkes Booth stole into the box. Booth, a fanatical Southern sympathiser and a melodramatic actor by profession, had joined in a conspiracy to murder the leading members of the government. As the last incident in a carefully planned campaign of hallucinatory revenge, he fired his pistol point blank at the President's head. Then he leapt over the front of the box and fell upon the stage shouting *"Sic Semper Tyrannis"* and was gone.[2]

Lincoln was mortally wounded. He made no sound or sign as they carried him down the stairs and across the road to a house and laid him upon a bed in a small room on the ground floor. His wife and family were there, and soon most members of the Cabinet and many others—too many—were in the room and in the house. It was about 10:45 p.m. when Lincoln was laid upon the bed in the small room. He died at a little after twenty past seven next morning, Saturday, April 15. The stout, great heart had ceased to beat.

Stanton, the Secretary of War, had stood for a long time by the bedside. It is told that when he heard that Lincoln was dead, he said: "Now be belongs to the ages." Whether he said it or not, it is suggested by Carl Sandburg, for example, that he was very ready to have it thought that he said it, and "by his wish [it] became legend beyond recall." We do not need to know whether these words were said, or if they were, who said them. But we may well consider whether they are true or not.

[2] He escaped on horseback; was caught at last on April 25 in Virginia, and, refusing to surrender, was shot and died on the morning of April 26. His fellow-conspirators were tried and punished by death or imprisonment. They had succeeded also in inflicting serious injuries by stabbing Seward, the Secretary of State, as he lay in bed at his home.

Abraham Lincoln did great things for his party, for his country and for the world. Yet what he himself would most have wished to do for his party died with him, if not before him. What he did for his country and for the world grows larger and clearer as the years go by. We must consider these things a little.

If anyone who had made no special study of American history were asked to say to which party he thought it likely that Abraham Lincoln belonged—the party of Franklin Roosevelt and Woodrow Wilson or the party of Herbert Hoover and Warren G. Harding, it is pretty certain that he would place Lincoln in the same party as Franklin Roosevelt and Woodrow Wilson, the two great Presidents of the United States since Lincoln. But he would not be right. The party of Hoover and Harding, the Republican party, is the party of Abraham Lincoln. He was the first President that that party provided for the United States and the greatest. He has been followed by a succession of Republican Presidents—with five exceptions—to this day, but no one of them has reached his stature. Some, like Theodore Roosevelt, have been men of unusual ability and great drive, others, like William H. Taft, have been men of integrity and good capacity. But the two greatest Presidents since Lincoln have been provided by the Democratic party.

The debt of the Republican party to Lincoln is great. He gave it a coherent policy on the slavery question at a time when it was in mortal danger from the attack of Douglas's popular sovereignty. His moderation where emancipation was concerned, his preference for compromise and compensation, and his determination above all to save the Union, gathered to the support of the Republican party solid backing which went far to ensure its success. Not that Lincoln at any time, even after his election to the Presidency, was powerful in the counsels of the party managers. His strength lay in the country, and particularly in states where the extremes of abolitionism and secession could not make the strongest appeal.

Yet when all this is said, the story of his Presidency is the story of his struggles with the leaders, particularly the Congressional leaders, of the Republicans, more than with the leaders of the Northern Democrats. There were those in his party who thought he was going too far, especially in the policy of the Emancipation Proclamation. They believed that the right to hold slaves in any state, rebel state or loyal state, should not be interfered with, and they held that the Republican party should adhere to this principle in spite of all that had happened in the Civil War. But it was from the anti-slavery enthusiasts that Lincoln received his greatest troubles. Some of the foulest things said against Lincoln were uttered by these enthusiasts.

Some of these divisions within the party showed themselves in 1864, when the time came again for the nomination of a candidate for the Presidential election. In particular a convention was called together at Cleveland, Ohio, on May 31, 1864, a week before the regular Republican convention was due to meet at Baltimore. Those who considered Lincoln too radical attempted to get General Grant nominated as Presidential candidate. They failed. Those who thought Lincoln too conservative succeeded in nominating Frémont. But after a few months no public support was forthcoming and Frémont withdrew from the contest. Lincoln himself was adopted at the Baltimore convention with overwhelming support.

But it is not surprising to know, in view of these differences of opinion, that, as Professor D. W. Brogan puts it in his *American Political System,* "Lincoln was scarcely safely buried before his sorrowing party was using his name to carry out policies which he would have fought to the end had he lived." And Lincoln himself would not have been surprised at this. He knew himself that in American history already party names had remained while party policies changed. He wrote something on this subject once, in a letter, dated April 6, 1859, to some people who had asked him to lecture at Boston in honour of Thomas Jefferson. In this letter he maintains that the Republicans in 1859 stand for what, in Jefferson's view, the Democrats stood in his day. And it is interesting to suggest that in our day the policy of the Democrats as Franklin Roosevelt expounded it is in line with the policy which Lincoln claimed and asserted for the Republicans.

"Remembering, too," he says, "that the Jefferson party was formed upon its supposed superior devotion to the rights of men, holding the rights of property to be secondary only, and greatly inferior, and assuming that the so-called Democracy of today are the Jefferson, and their opponents, the anti-Jefferson party, it will be equally interesting to note how completely the two have changed hands as to the principle upon which they were originally supposed to be divided. The Democrats of today hold the liberty of one man to be absolutely nothing, when in conflict with another man's right of property; Republicans, on the contrary, are for both the man and the dollar, but in case of conflict the man before the dollar.

"I remember being once much amused at seeing two partially intoxicated men engaged in a fight with their greatcoats on, which fight, after a long and harmless contest, ended in each having fought himself out of his own coat and into that of the other. If the two leading parties of this day are really identical with the two in the days of Jefferson and Adams, they have performed the same feat as the two drunken men."

Lincoln would not have been surprised, though he might have been distressed, to find that it was his own party, the Republicans, of which it was more just to say what he himself said of the Democrats in his day, that they hold the liberty of one man to be absolutely nothing, when in conflict with another man's right of property. It was Franklin Roosevelt, the Democrat, not Herbert Hoover, the Republican, who could claim to be the heir of Abraham Lincoln and of his belief that the Republican party should show devotion for the personal rights of men, holding the rights of property to be secondary only; for the man and the dollar, but in case of conflict, the man before the dollar. So once more, after a long though perhaps not entirely "harmless" contest, the two great parties had fought themselves into each other's greatcoats.

Signs that Lincoln's policies died with him were soon apparent. When the period of reconstruction opened, with the close of the war, the principles that guided it were not those of Abraham Lincoln. Not that his successor, Andrew Johnson, the Vice-President, advocated a different policy. On the contrary, his plan for reconstruction, put forth in a proclamation of May 29, 1865, was said by Seward, Lincoln's Secretary of State, to have grown during the administration of Lincoln, and it appears to resemble closely a plan which had been considered in the Cabinet on the last day of Lincoln's life. But Congress would have none of it. Not all the blame for the failure of Lincoln's plans must be laid upon his untimely death and the succession of Andrew Johnson. It is true that Johnson was a man of weaker fibre than Lincoln, but he had against him a Congress which although Republican was strong in opposition to moderate policies, and it is fair to say that Lincoln himself could not have prevailed against them. The radical vindictives, whose views had been embodied already in the Wade-Davis Bill, soon had charge of Congress.

When all this is said and considered, it is pardonable to say that the greatest legacy Lincoln left to his party was the crown of martyrdom. In truth his great achievements were too big to be claimed as the private property of any party, though inevitably the Republicans staked their claim and could not possibly be prevented from enjoying some of the fame. But the two great achievements of Abraham Lincoln—what he did to save the Union, and what he did to defend and assert democratic government—transcend party, and, indeed, in their remoter consequences, transcend his own country. Abraham Lincoln did more than any other single man to preserve the American Union, to remake the United States and to state in imperishable language the harder truths of democracy. And in a world where, twice since Lincoln's time, the United States has intervened outside its borders in a struggle for freedom and democracy, it is not difficult to see that what Lincoln did then has its influence and beneficent effects in later centuries and in larger climes than his own.

To say this is not to say that Lincoln was the only man who saved the Union, nor that it could not have been saved without him, nor that he never made mistakes; nor is it to deny that had he lived his reputation and his work might not have escaped without serious criticism and some considerable measure of failure. But it is the life that he was permitted to live that we consider and upon which we pronounce. He was a great man—great in courage, great in charity, great in simplicity and great in the power of speaking the truth of liberty and equality to the people. In these things "now he belongs to the ages."

Further Reading

I. The most complete and accurate source collection for the story of Lincoln's career and administration is Roy P. Basler, ed., *Abraham Lincoln, Collected Works* (9 vols., 1953–1955). This work has almost completely superseded the somewhat unreliable collection by John G. Nicolay and John Hay, *The Complete Works of Abraham Lincoln* (12 vols., 1905). The Hay and Nicolay *Abraham Lincoln: A History* (10 vols., 1890) is still an important source. In recent times various smaller collections of Lincoln's speeches and writings have been published. Next to Basler's *Collected Works*, his *Abraham Lincoln, His Speeches and Writings* (1946) is the most accurate text.

II. Lincoln's life must be studied in the light of the American history that preceded and followed him. One of the best general histories for this purpose is S. E. Morison and H. S. Commager, *The Growth of the American Republic* (5th ed., 1962). On the history of the period immediately surrounding Lincoln's life and work, James G. Randall's enthralling book *The Civil War and Reconstruction* (2nd ed., 1953).

The careful student of the Lincoln period should be aware of some of the classic works in American history. Among these are: Edward Channing, *A History of the United States* (6 vols., 1905–1925), especially vol. VI; John B. McMaster, *A History of the People of the United States During Lincoln's Administration* (1927); James Ford Rhodes, *History of the United States From The Compromise of 1850* (7 vols., 1893–1906), especially vols. 3, 4, 5; and his *History of the Civil War* (1917), especially chaps. 4, 5, 8, 9.

A popular but substantial account of Lincoln's war administration is Burton J. Hendrick, *Lincoln's War Cabinet* (1946). Some other important modern accounts are: Jay Monaghan, *Diplomat in Carpet Slippers: Abraham Lincoln Deals with Foreign Affairs* (1945); Allan Nevins, *The Emergence of Lincoln* (2 vols., 1950), especially vol. I, chaps. 15,

16, and vol. II, chap. 11; also Nevins' *Ordeal of the Union* (2 vols., 1947); Roy F. Nichols, *Disruption of American Democracy* (1948), which is now available in a 1962 Collier Books Edition (BS 49); Avery O. Craven, *The Coming of the Civil War* (2nd ed., 1957), especially chaps. 16, 17; Arthur C. Cole, *The Irrepressible Conflict, 1850–1865* (1934), especially chaps. 13, 14; and Kenneth M. Stampp, *And The War Came* (1950).

III. Carl Sandburg has written the fullest of all biographies of Lincoln; its style is imaginative, its wealth of detail enormous. Almost everything any student could be interested in is touched upon somewhere in its six volumes. Opinions will differ about its merits; in my opinion it is a great panorama of a book, which every student should consult—published as *Abraham Lincoln: The Prairie Years* (2 vols., 1926) and *Abraham Lincoln: The War Years* (4 vols., 1939); Carl Sandburg, *Abraham Lincoln, The Prairie Years and The War Years* (a one volume abridgement of the six volume work published in 1956).

James G. Randall was the greatest modern scholar in the Lincoln field. His *Lincoln: The President* (4 vols., 1945–1955) takes the story of Lincoln's presidency to the Gettysburg speech, and it was completed (the fourth volume) by Richard N. Current. Mention should also be made of Professor Randall's *Lincoln, The Liberal Statesman* (1949) and his *Constitutional Problems Under Lincoln*.

In addition, the reader may want to consult some of the following works: Paul M. Angle, *A Shelf of Lincoln Books: A Critical Selective Bibliography of Lincolniana* (1946)—useful, but somewhat outdated; Paul M. Angle, ed., *The Lincoln Reader* (1947)—a skillfully written anthology of biographical material concerning Lincoln, including both contemporaries and later writers; Benjamin P. Thomas, *Abraham Lincoln, A Biography* (1952)—scholarly and very well-written; *Portrait For Posterity: Lincoln and his Biographers* (1947)—penetrating estimates of attitudes and outlooks, especially of Lincoln's early biographers; Richard N. Current, *Mr. Lincoln* (1957)—this is a one-volume condensation of Randall's biography; and Roy P. Basler, *The Lincoln Legend*

(1935)—an analysis of the creation of the national Lincoln legend or myth.

IV. The most complete Lincoln Bibliographies can be found in: Jay Monaghan, compiler, *A Lincoln Bibliography* (2 vols., 1943–45) and David C. Mearns, *The Lincoln Papers* (2 vols., 1948).

Index